UNDERSTANDING
FRESHWATER
FISH

UNDERSTANDING
FRESHWATER
FISH

DICK MILLS

Howell Book House

Credits

Created and designed: Ideas into Print,
New Ash Green, Kent DA3 8JD, UK.
Computer graphics: Phil Holmes and
Stuart Watkinson
Production management: Consortium,
Poslingford, Suffolk CO10 8RA, UK.
Print production: Sino Publishing
House Ltd., Hong Kong.
Printed and bound in China.

The author

Dick Mills, author of many aquarium
books, is a former editor of The Aquarist
& Pondkeeper magazine and also a Vice-
President of the Federation of British
Aquatic Societies. He has kept aquarium
and pond fish continuously for the last
40 years, but also finds time to travel,
when – as if by accident – he always
manages to come across a public
aquarium or two.

*Below: A typical lowland river rich in
plant and aquatic life, including healthy
populations of native coldwater fish.*

Contents

Introduction

It is said that man differs from other animals in one or two ways; apparently, no other animals laugh but, on the other hand, no animals hunt or kill other species just for the 'fun' of it. Another human characteristic, perhaps more relevant in the context of this book, is man's appreciation of beauty and a desire to learn about other living things.

In this respect, the coldwater fish has a lot to answer for. From the days when it was first captured and confined as a food source, it has also appealed to man's aesthetic nature and provided a source of visual pleasure and wonderment.

It is quite true that the majority of fishkeepers, whilst totally appreciative of their fishes' decorative qualities, never feel the need to understand what actually goes on in the depths of their garden ponds or indoor aquariums. They know little of the fish's struggle to live in its environment. How do fish cope with all the variations in water conditions, how and where do they breed, and where do they find their food? And, more importantly, how can they ensure that they do not become food themselves?

If you are only familiar with the ubiquitous goldfish or koi, you may be surprised to learn that there are 'plenty of other fish in the sea', with highly specialized physical characteristics and evolved behavioural patterns that allow them to live their particular lives to the full.

This book will open your eyes to another world and – especially if you are already a fishkeeper – give you an insight into how you can provide the best conditions for the fish in your care. Then, all you need do is sit back and enjoy the wonderful world of coldwater fish.

WHAT IS A COLDWATER FISH?

Before tropical fishkeeping became a popular hobby, people only kept coldwater fish – and for sound practical reasons. In this chapter, we define what is meant by the term 'coldwater fish' and how the hobby has developed.

The water of life

From the moment water hits the ground as rain and accumulates, life-forms will inhabit it. This happens even in these fast-flowing torrents.

The term 'coldwater fish' is both difficult and easy to define – it all depends on your viewpoint and, a great deal, on your geographical location. Obviously, the term was created at some stage since the study and culture of fishkeeping began, but it seems unlikely that there is a 'set in stone' definition that can be applied to all instances.

For one thing, there is certainly no clear 'cut-off' point delineated by taxonomic families, as many families (and the genera contained within them) often inhabit waters of all temperatures. Neither can we accept without question that fish requiring unheated aquariums fall into this category; one has only to think of the ambient water temperatures in subtropical and tropical countries – where it is not uncommon for fishes from all water temperatures to be kept in the same

Above: Beneath the surface of the water, the continuing cycle of aquatic life is always evident. Plant life provides sanctuary, food and spawning sites, so that young fish can mature and breed.

aquarium – to see the emptiness of this argument. Furthermore, it is often difficult to appreciate that, for many people, there is no such thing as coldwater fishes or coldwater fishkeeping, unless we modify the basic definition to include fish that require artificially cooled water to sustain them!

It might be feasible to claim that fishes found naturally between certain latitudes conform to our definition but, with contemporary climatic variations, we could not be sure how long the list would remain accurate. Perhaps we should look at

things from a different point of view and categorize coldwater fishes as those species capable of naturally surviving temperatures below a certain value.

It seems, therefore, that this category of fishes is an entirely artificial group created by us for our own convenience. Turning from science, let us look at what fishkeepers generally accept as coldwater fishes.

To those fishkeepers living in temperate zones of the world, it means fishes that can be kept in any container filled with water (pond or aquarium) without recourse to heating. (Paradoxically, this often includes so-called 'tropical' species with a lower temperature tolerance than their more warmth-loving relatives.) In terms of species or

Above: *The salmon,* Salmo salar, *inhabits both fresh and salt waters during its most complex and dramatic life, adapting to the severest changes in water conditions.*

varieties, this is taken to mean cultivated, 'manmade' fishes, such as goldfish, orfe and koi, together with many naturally found species native to northern America, continental Europe, China and Japan.

As the Cyprinidae family is the largest group of fishes in the world, it should come as no surprise that a good many of its members inhabit coldwater areas. Other representative contributing families include the Cobitidae, Cottidae, Centrarchidae, Gasterosteidae and Siluridae.

Although all the fishes mentioned so far are freshwater species, we should not forget that many marine fishes from equally temperate conditions can also be kept in captivity. For example, blennies and gobies from local seashore rockpools often make excellent 'coldwater' aquarium subjects. This book will be mostly concerned with species from freshwater environments although, where necessary (or as an added point of interest), related characteristics found in marine species will also be included.

How it all started

The desire to keep fish as decorative subjects was most certainly not the factor that gave rise to modern, or even ancestral, fishkeeping. The most pressing requirement was the need for fresh food. If people happened to live far from the seashore, their chances of enjoying fresh fish were very slim indeed; with only primitive transportation at their disposal, purveyors of food would have found a very limited distribution area for their produce, given the non-existence of refrigeration or any other forms of food preservation methods. Fresh fish might be caught from local lakes and rivers but, in the main, fish was not necessarily high on the average menu.

This would have changed with the coming of Christianity, in which many days of the year were designated as being 'meat-free'. As a result, the demand for an appetizing alternative to meat may have triggered a rise in fish consumption and, subsequently, its production and more widespread supply.

It is, therefore, highly likely that the defensive moat systems found around villages were also used (in more settled, non-violent times) to house live fish for convenient consumption. A typical example of this would be the stew-ponds found in monasteries. (Stew-pond is a Middle English term derived from the French 'estui', from estoier meaning 'to confine'.) The Roman legions would not, for instance, have ventured very far eastwards if they had not been sustained by fish caught from the River Danube. As piscinae were already established in Rome for the exhibition of sea fishes by wealthy citizens displaying the latest 'house-fashion' accessory, it is not inconceivable that carp may well have been brought home by the Roman army and kept alive (and probably bred naturally) in such enclosures, now filled with fresh water to sustain them.

From these beginnings, it only requires a short leap of the imagination to visualize a more caring 'keeper of the fishes' becoming upset should a favourite fish be selected for the table. He would also have noticed any deviation in coloration, shape or size amongst his charges. Naturally, a more highly coloured specimen would stand out amongst the other, usually drab, inmates, and this fish may well have

Left: *Could this be an early record of fishkeeping? This Egyptian fresco in the tomb of Nebamun at Thebes dating from 1400 BC shows an ornamental pond containing fish, waterfowl and plants.*

Above: *In this typically European scene (circa 1500), the moat surrounding the settlement could well have changed use from being a defensive barrier to a provider of fresh fish for the table.*

been segregated from the rest to enjoy a peaceful 'retirement' and less useful end to its days.

Illustrative literature shows quite clearly that ornamental fish were revered in China as long ago as AD 1000, with the carp (probably goldfish) held in particularly high esteem. However, the arrival and establishment of decorative coldwater fish was not to reach the Western world for a few more hundred years. It is a fact that the appreciation of the coldwater fish had to travel even further eastwards, to Japan, in about 1500 before retracing its steps (and beyond) to reach Europe around the seventeenth century and the New World in the 1870s.

In Japan, the storing of carp in ponds probably alternated with the cultivation of rice in paddy-fields. At the now traditionally recognized home of koi, in Niigata Province, ponds were covered with thick layers of snow during the long winters, and it is likely that fish living in the dark waters would have developed darker-coloured patterning as a result. These fish, in turn, would have been marked out as something special, isolated from the less attractive specimens and reared to form breeding stock from which more coloured variants would emerge. In this way, the elements of today's koi-keeping were established.

Coldwater fishkeeping today

Although it is fair to say that many species of coldwater fishes are kept throughout the world, the strongest following is amongst the keepers of just two species: *Carassius auratus* and *Cyprinus carpio*.

The humble goldfish, *Carassius auratus*, may well be but one species, but such is its attraction, and value as genetic raw material, that many variants have been developed by enthusiastic fishkeepers over the centuries.

Similarly, the koi (the Japanese word for carp), *Cyprinus carpio*, has also enjoyed many years of development. The results of intense koi breeding programmes now attempt to supply the voracious demands of fishkeepers across the world.

There are national bodies in several countries whose members are devoted keepers of these fishes and, as a result, many countries

Left: *There is no mistaking the fish theme painted on this exquisitely shaped oriental vase. It clearly reflects the respect in which carp have long been held.*

Above: *Modern fishkeepers would question the desirability of keeping goldfish in such a tiny bowl, but there is no denying its charm and beauty.*

Above: Visitors to this koi show gather around the show vats to admire and compare the merits of the colourful fish on display. Note the photographs to aid the identification of different varieties.

Left: This Showa Sanke is an excellent example of the fine coloration patterns found in koi. Note how they are confined to the sides and upper surface of the fish to facilitate pond viewing from above.

outside those in which the fish were first developed now have thriving goldfish and koi breeding industries.

This is not to decry the keeping of lesser-known coldwater species and, whilst these species may not generally rival tropical species for coloration, they are well worth keeping nonetheless.

Where do they come from?

It seems that wherever there is enough water to swim, there you will find fish. Every natural watercourse flows downstream, from initial streams to final wide-mouthed estuaries, and the aquatic animals at each point have adapted to the prevailing water conditions. At the extreme end of the lower temperature range, fish are even found in the Antarctic, where their bloodstream contains almost the equivalent of antifreeze to keep it flowing. Beyond doubt, such species are truly coldwater specimens!

Sizes and colours

In general, coldwater fishes are larger but less colourful than tropical species, with the obvious exception of the non-naturally-occurring species, such as the cultivated varieties already mentioned.

The difference in physical size is due to the increased amount of oxygen available in colder water, which enables the fish to develop faster. Brilliant colours are not a feature of coldwater fishes, as many spend their lives in turbid, murky waters, where such attractive garb would not be an advantage and would, in any case, pass completely unrecognized. The main apparel comprises a countershading pattern, with the upper surface of the body being a greenish brown, shading progressively to lighter tones down the flanks to a silver-white underbelly.

This arrangement protects the fish from detection by predators from above and below, as the dark colours camouflage it against the dark riverbed and the light colour 'loses' the fish against the brighter background of the sky. Additionally, as the light source in any natural

Below: All goldfish start out having drab dark brown coloration. Towards the end of their first year, generally from around nine months onwards, the gold colour spreads upwards from the belly. However, not every goldfish changes colour.

body of water always comes from above, the countershading design tends to flatten out all determining coloration from the fish when seen from the side so that it loses its 'fish shape' outline very effectively.

This begs the question "Where did the colours of goldfish and koi came from?" In answering it, we must acknowledge the tremendous amount of work and effort undertaken by fish breeders across the years. The present day's supplies of colourful variants have emerged from isolated cases of naturally occurring colour 'sports'. Yet, such is the delicate balance between natural and manmade designs that it would take only a brief period of time (relatively speaking) for all those varieties to revert to their original, less vibrant colorations should they be returned to the wild once more.

Left: *This aquarium-developed moor is jet black in colour, with protruding 'telescopic' eyes and ornate finnage, none of which would be found on a natural fish.*

Above: *It seems almost incomprehensible that so many colour varieties, body shapes and finnages could come from a single species. Ongoing efforts to produce yet another strain show that coldwater fishkeeping still has a long life ahead of it.*

How coldwater fish work

Coldwater fish can find their way and locate their daily food in a cold, dark and wet environment without bumping into other fish or colliding with obstacles in their path. This section explains in full detail how they do it.

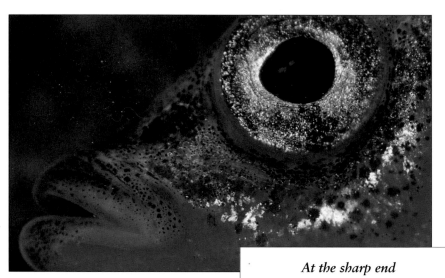

Everyone knows what shape a fish is; in general, it has a pointed snout at the front and a tail fin at the rear. In between there is a streamlined body that may be cylindrical in shape or either depressed horizontally or compressed laterally. The body not only has to accommodate the vital organs inside, but must be suitably designed to operate in water.

The fins

The fins are equivalent to the limbs of a terrestrial animal. They are composed of stiff rays that support

At the sharp end

The snout of a fish is fully equipped for locating food – using its eyes, nostrils and taste sensors – and for consuming it – using the jaws.

the tissue spread across them. Fish usually have a basic set of seven fins – three single and two paired fins. However, some fish, such as salmon, trout and catfish, have an extra small fin – composed mainly of fat – situated behind the dorsal fin, on top of the caudal peduncle and ahead of the caudal fin. This is the adipose fin, but its exact purpose is not known.

The two paired fins, pectoral and pelvic, towards the front of the fish, correspond to arms and legs and are used to control manoeuvring movements – upwards, downwards, braking, maintaining position, etc. However, they can also be used during breeding to direct currents of water to wherever they may be needed. At breeding time, too, the pectoral fins of some male fish become stiffened and carry visible tubercles like those found on the gill covers of cyprinid fishes (see pages 66 and 67). In some cases, the pectoral fins may be further strengthened to assist 'walking' on the substrate, and pelvic fins (incidentally, totally absent in eels) are often combined to act as a sucker disc to anchor the fish in position.

The median fins (median meaning middle-line) are all aligned vertically: the dorsal and anal fins reduce any sideways rolling movements. In male fishes, the dorsal fin may carry extended rays or become more pointed (a useful guide to positive sexual identification). In some species, the anal fin is occasionally used as a spawning aid. The tail fin, usually referred to as the caudal fin, provides thrust for forward movement. By looking at the construction of the caudal fin,

The full set of fins

This goldfish has the typical set of fins found in most coldwater fishes.

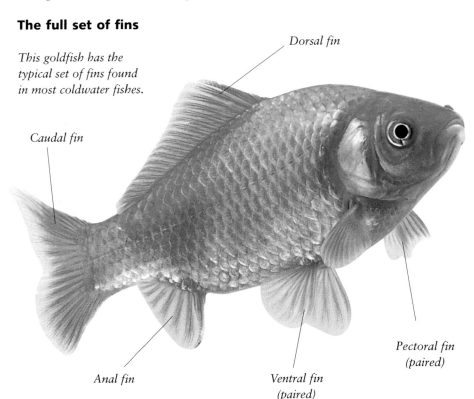

Dorsal fin

Caudal fin

Pectoral fin (paired)

Anal fin

Ventral fin (paired)

which may be spade-shaped, deeply cleft or even asymmetrical, you can pick up clues to the fish's normal style of movement. Paddle-shaped caudal fins make for short bursts of speed, while the thin, crescent forms are a feature of the 'sustained speed merchants' of the underwater world.

Body coverings

Scales, the small plates covering the fish's skin, are overlaid in such a way that they provide the least resistance to the water that flows from the head of the fish backwards along its body. This is just as important to the fish as the protection provided by the scales against injury and wounds. However, sheathing the entire body in rigid scales would result in a very inflexible body, so scales are only attached to the body through the skin at their front edge or apex; this produces a hinged effect, and the overlapping, roof-tile arrangement of all the scales allows the fish to twist and flex the body as required. Depending on species, scales may be of three types: ganoid, ctenoid or cycloid.

Types of scales

Ganoid scales are made of an enamel-like material (ganoine) and are four-sided and equipped with tiny teeth. They are mostly found on primitive fishes such as the garpikes and bichirs.

Ctenoid scales are smoother, but have comblike teeth on the rear edges, while cycloid scales are similarly smooth with round rear edges. (It is possible to find both ctenoid and cycloid scales on the same fish and, in some cases, smoother ctenoid scales and rougher

Left: Cycloid scales, found on the majority of fishes, have smooth rear edges. Like all scales, they are attached to the fish through the skin at a single point, creating an overlapping covering that flexes with the movements of the body.

cycloid scales often make exact scale definition difficult.) The fish's age may be determined by counting the number of growth rings on the scale in a similar manner to dating trees by counting the rings on a cross-section of their trunks.

In some fishes, the scales may be so minute as to give the fish a naked appearance; in others, notably the sturgeon and sterlet (*Acipenser* spp.), the scales may be replaced by protective bony plates called scutes.

Fish are provided with further protection, in this case against invasion by disease, by a mucus coating covering the scales; this also contributes to a reduction in friction as the fish moves through the water and lubricates the scales as they move over each other. It is a long-standing belief (as yet unproven) that the mucus found on the skin of the

tench *(Tinca tinca)* has healing properties and that other fish suffering from wounds or ailments often rub against the tench to be cured. An alternative explanation is that the tench is actually transferring parasites from its own skin to sick fish, which are easier to parasitize than healthy ones.

How fishes move
Contrary to belief, the side-to-side movement of the caudal fin is not the sole factor that contributes to the fish's forward movement through water. In fact, it is the final action of muscular power developed much further forward on the body. Muscle segments (myotomes) on each side of the body alternately expand and contract, producing a rippling effect down the body that discharges its energy through a vigorous sweep of

Below: A close-up view of these scales belonging to the garpike reveals that they are four-sided ganoid scales typically found in more primitive fishes. They form a sturdy but flexible suit of armour.

Above: These ctenoid scales have typical comblike fringes along the trailing edges. They are similar to cycloid scales and may appear with them on the same fish.

the caudal fin. This is the standard form of propulsive power generated in all fish, but there are certain refinements. For example, the eel has no caudal fin worthy of propulsion-generating note and in this case the whole body is pressed into service as the propellant. The eel's sinuous swimming movement is not only confined to water, but is also used when the eel makes any overland journeys. The edges of the scales on the underside of the body grip the ground and thus provide additional

Below: This photograph of a shoal of red shiners has captured various stages of the sequential 'head-to-tail' bodily muscular action that generates forward movement. Clearly, more than just the tail is involved.

traction. The amount of muscle also defines the speed of the fish; a goldfish's muscles may comprise nearly half its body weight, but fast swimmers, especially those in marine waters, may well devote nearly three-quarters of the body to muscle.

However, not all fish use muscular 'wave power' to propel themselves through the water. Flatfishes and rays do use 'wave motion' but it is generated by fins fringing the whole body. Other marine species use just the opposing dorsal and anal fins, while the seahorse manages with just the dorsal fin.

How colour is used and produced
Why would a fish need colour when colours progressively disappear as the water deepens? There are several answers to this.

Species recognition by patterning is one obvious reason (it is a great

Above: Cryptic coloration, here shown in a Cottus gobio, *usually camouflages the fish against the substrate for one of two basic reasons: self-protection or for predatory feeding purposes.*

help to the fishkeeper, too!) Camouflage seems another good purpose, whether this is by mimicking the surrounding colours or by deliberately forming a disruptive pattern, disguising the fish's actual shape. Dressing up during courtship is not a habit peculiar to the terrestrial world either. Colour can also be used for defensive purposes; some species display decoy patterns to lead an attacker's attention say, to a false eye and thus away from the real thing. Colour also helps to protect the fish from ultraviolet radiation by screening out these harmful rays. Finally, in an almost unprecedented

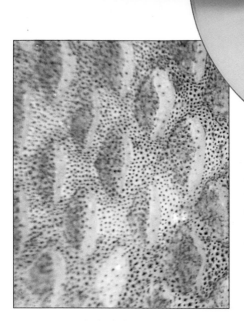

Above: The virtual colours on a CD are caused by light dispersal in the same way as iridocytes create colour under the skin.

Left: The colour pigmentation cells, or chromatophores, can be clearly seen in the skin. By expanding or contracting these, the fish can darken or lighten the overall intensity of its coloration.

display of civic duty, some fish announce the fact that their skin is toxic by exhibiting gaudy colours. It obviously pays to advertise if it prevents being eaten.

The basic countershading colour pattern described earlier may also be helpful in deterring predators. In a shoal of similarly coloured fish it is hard for an attacker to pick out any individual member, and a sudden turn (followed by a rapid dispersal) by the whole shoal could momentarily dazzle or shock the attacker, allowing a fish to escape (see the photograph on page 56-7).

Colour is produced in two ways: by pigmentation or by reflective materials beneath the skin. Pigmentation cells, or chromatophores, are made up of melanophores (black), xanthophores (yellow) and erythrophores (red). Combinations of these basic elements result in different colours and also

shading effects. Some fish have direct control over the chromatophores; contracting them makes the colours fade, expansion makes them brighter.

The metallic sheen seen in most coldwater fishes is brought about by iridocytes (guanophores) in the skin. Guanin, a waste product, is laid down as crystals beneath the scales, where it reflects the light penetrating through the scales back out again. Depending on the angle at which the light falls onto the fish, the degree and coloration of the metallic effect are correspondingly affected.

The best examples of colour and metallic sheens are found in goldfish varieties. Here, too, the amount of guanin found beneath the scales is responsible for the three scalation types recognized by goldfish keepers: metallic (full guanin), nacreous (less guanin) and matt (no guanin). In the latter case, the lack of guanin allows more of the skin pigments to show

Variations on a reflective theme

Metallic scales Layers of iridocytes (guanin crystals) beneath each scale and in the dermis itself give the goldfish its characteristic metallic sheen.

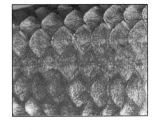

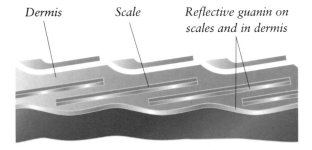

Dermis   *Scale*   *Reflective guanin on scales and in dermis*

All the light reflecting back from the iridocytes creates a totally solid sheen to the fish.

Nacreous scales Here, iridocytes are just present in the dermis and can only shine through a limited amount, giving a 'mother of pearl' appearance.

Guanin is restricted to a layer beneath the dermis

As the amount of iridocytes is reduced, a more random degree of sheen is produced.

Matt scales With no iridocytes beneath the scales or in the dermis, scales appear to be transparent and coloration is provided by pigmentation cells alone.

No reflective guanin on scales or in dermis

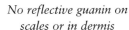

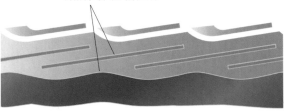

No iridocytes at all give the fish a naked look, only relieved by the chromatophores.

How does a fish hear under water?

Otoliths ('ear stones') in the inner ear vibrate against hair cells that generate nerve impulses. These travel to the brain and are 'heard' as sound.

These linking bones transfer the sound vibrations to the inner ear.

The swimbladder vibrates in response to sound waves transmitted through the body tissues. The gas in the bladder amplifies the sound vibrations.

Sound travels through water as a series of vibrations.

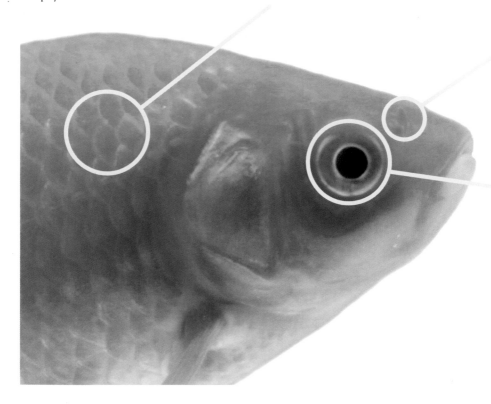

How the nostrils work

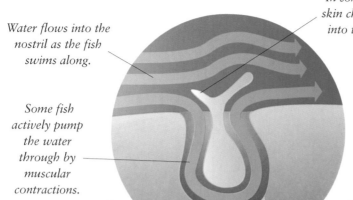

Water flows into the nostril as the fish swims along.

In some fish, a flap of skin channels the water into the front nostril.

Some fish actively pump the water through by muscular contractions.

Receptor cells respond to dissolved substances and generate nerve impulses interpreted by the brain as smell.

Inside a fish's eye

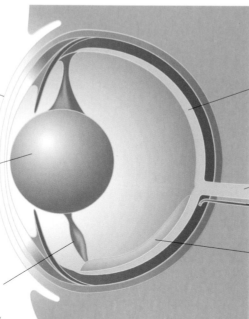

The cornea – a thin sandwich of transparent layers.

The retina converts images into nerve impulses.

The lens remains roughly spherical at all focus ranges.

The optic nerve carries these 'images' to the brain.

This muscle moves the lens to focus images on the retina.

Blood supply to the retina.

The falciform process distributes blood around the retina.

through and accounts for the range of colours found in such varieties as the Bristol and London shubunkin. 'Pearl essence', a product made from the guanin found on the scales of the bleak *(Alburnus alburnus)* was once used to coat glass beads in the manufacture of artificial pearls.

Vision in water

Bearing in mind the varied water conditions that fish may encounter (which in some cases may make sight worthless anyway), sight is probably less important to a fish than a good sense of smell.

With eyes situated on each side of the head, a fish is unlikely to enjoy true binocular vision, although where the eyes are set high up and closer together this may be available to some species. However, the fact that the lens is spherical (the best shape for an object subjected to underwater pressure) and projects through the iris means that the fish has excellent wide-angle vision – indeed, genuine 'fish-eye' coverage, albeit limited to fairly short distances. Being permanently immersed in water, there is no need for the protective and lubricating eyelid found in terrestrial animals, and the method of focusing is different, too. Fish vary the focal length of the eye by moving the lens forward and back (to and fro in the direction of the head and tail) rather than by altering its curvature, as happens in terrestrial animals. A combination of rods and cones in the retina convert light into nerve impulses and provide an image of the underwater world. The rods are very

sensitive but only work in monochrome and are found in greater numbers in the retinas of deepwater fish. The cones need higher light levels to 'fire' and provide colour vision.

The sense of smell

As the fish's environment is in water, the senses of smell and taste are geared to deal with dissolved substances. In this respect it is not always easy to see where the two senses part company. One suggestion put forward is that smell is more concerned with long range sensing, while taste is for much closer items.

Fish have nostrils but, unlike those of humans, these do not form any part in respiration. The nostrils are

situated in pairs above the mouth, and water passes through them continuously by independent circulatory means in conjunction with the breathing movements of the jaw and operculum below, or simply as the fish's movement through the water pushes water through them.

The sense of smell varies from species to species. That of the eel (like the shark) is excellent, whereas the pike depends on its eyesight, lightning acceleration and a large mouth when seeking prey.

Salmon use their sense of smell to locate their 'home' river when returning from the sea to spawn and actually locate the very creek where they themselves first began life. (See pages 72-74 for more on this.)

Taste and touch

A fish need not always have food in its mouth in order to taste it, as the sense of taste in fish is not limited to taste sensors in the mouth. There are other taste sensors located over exterior parts of the body, too. Some fish have barbels growing around the mouth, and these fleshy appendages are used in turbid waters not only to detect obstacles but also to 'taste' whatever they encounter. Taste buds can also be found on pectoral and pelvic fins in some marine and

Below: The flattened ventral surface allows the taste-sensitive barbels around the mouth of this Chinese rainbow loach (Micronemacheilichthys pulcher) *to come into close contact with the substrate.*

tropical species. Chemicals such as pheromones produced by some fish can also be detected by sensors on the body, and the effects of these are discussed on page 56.

The sense of touch is obviously present in fishes but, as described above, this sense is certainly more closely allied to taste than it is in terrestrial animals.

Hearing under water

Just as the 'smell' and 'taste' senses are inextricably intertwined, so describing the fish's sense of hearing can also be difficult. Since fish are sensitive to very low frequencies, the threshold between 'feeling' a vibration and actually hearing a sound is not clearly definable.

Whereas the human ear consists of the outer, middle and inner ear, in a fish there is no external connection, only the inner part. This inner ear, a labyrinthine sac filled with fluid, contains calcareous stones known as otoliths that transmit received vibrations to sheets of haircells, which in turn convert them to nerve impulses sent to the brain. (The otoliths grow each year and the age of the fish can be determined by examining the visible growth segments on them.) Semicircular canals extending from the sac provide fish with the sense of balance, as they do in our ears.

Variations in water pressure, due to changes in depth as the fish swims, affect the swimbladder. These can be 'audited' by the inner ear in cyprinid fishes due to a connecting mechanism of bony ossicles between the swimbladder and the inner ear. In this instance, the swimbladder acts both as a detector and an amplifier.

Fish have yet another mechanism for detecting pressure changes in their surrounding environment – the lateral line system. The row of tiny 'portholes' seen along the flanks of a fish are in fact apertures through the centres of a row of scales leading to a mucus-filled canal in which lie sensor cells called neuromasts. Differences in pressure generated in the surrounding water by movements of other fish, or reflections of the fish's own movement sent back from obstacles are all detected and the information sent to the fish's brain. This allows the fish to 'map out' its immediate vicinity, a very convenient aid during hours of darkness or in turbid water conditions.

Not all fish have a complete lateral line, while in others, such as tench and minnows, the 'line' may extend over the head. It is likely that salmon make good use of the lateral line system to detect when the moment is exactly right – in terms of minimum waterflow – to make that leap up a waterfall en route to their spawning grounds.

Digestive system

The intake and processing of food follows very much the same pattern as in mammalian life, with one or two slight differences.

Food enters the mouth, where it passes over the non-protrusible tongue and is blocked – and diverted into the gullet – by the gill rakers (see page 42). Fish have no need of

How the lateral line system works

Left: *Look closely at the flanks of a fish and you will see a line of pores running from head to tail. These are the openings to the lateral line, a sensory organ system that responds to pressure waves and gives the fish awareness of nearby objects.*

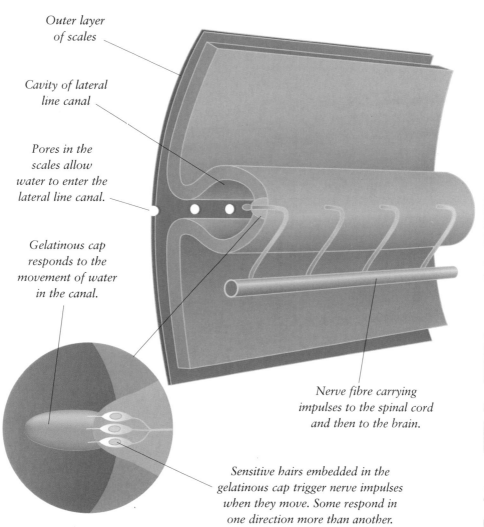

Outer layer of scales

Cavity of lateral line canal

Pores in the scales allow water to enter the lateral line canal.

Gelatinous cap responds to the movement of water in the canal.

Nerve fibre carrying impulses to the spinal cord and then to the brain.

Sensitive hairs embedded in the gelatinous cap trigger nerve impulses when they move. Some respond in one direction more than another.

salivary glands. While teeth play their usual role in cutting and grinding food – the pike has rows of movable teeth that allow one-way traffic only – not all fish have teeth in the jaws. Cyprinid fishes grind their food by moving pharyngeal teeth against a horny pad at the base of the skull.

A further feature of cyprinid fishes is that they have no stomach; their digestive tract is a continuous organ. This can give rise to problems, as they give the impression that they are always eating (or hungry). Food may well be taken, but unless it actually needs to be digested it passes straight through the fish and into the water where, unnoticed by the fishkeeper, it begins to pollute the water. A further complication arises at change-of-season times. After the winter, the fish's digestive system will not start to function at its maximum efficiency until the water temperature rises, and remains consistently above 10°C (50°F). Providing high-protein food during early spring and autumn may result in incomplete digestion, with the uneaten food being passed out of the fish's system. At these times, it is recommended practice to feed more easily digestible, wheatgerm-based foods. Feeding during winter is not a good idea, because while the fish is in a dormant state any food taken in will lie undigested in the gut, causing the fish even more problems.

The length of intestine varies depending on the fish's preferred diet. Carnivores (although it might be more correct to say piscivores) have fairly short, straight intestines, whereas those with a vegetarian tendency have much longer, more

Blood circulation

Oxygenated blood delivers oxygen to the tissues and carries away their waste products.

As blood passes through the gills it takes up oxygen and loses carbon dioxide.

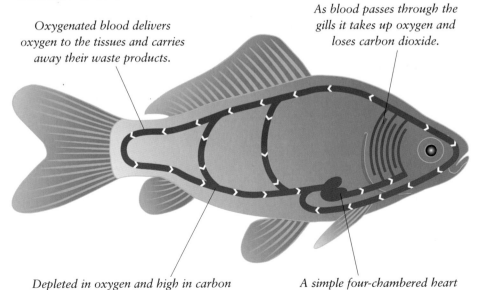

Depleted in oxygen and high in carbon dioxide, the blood returns to the heart.

A simple four-chambered heart pumps blood around the body.

Above: The pink, blood-rich gill filaments can be clearly seen through the gill cover of this shubunkin. This is a vital exchange zone for oxygen and waste materials.

coiled intestines. Once absorption of the food is complete, waste products are expelled at the anus. It is worth noting that fish do not have a cloaca – a combined urinary-gastro-genital opening. Each system has its own separate exit.

Blood circulation

Blood is distributed around the body for several purposes: it collects and carries vital oxygen to the body tissues while simultaneously disposing of waste products. It also distributes nutrients from the digestion system to the muscles. Starting at the heart, blood flows to the gills to pick up oxygen (and to dispose of carbon dioxide and ammonia). From the gills, the blood flows along two large arteries. One, the carotid, supplies blood to the head region, while the other, the dorsal aorta, distributes blood rearwards to all other parts of the body. Depleted of oxygen, but laden with waste products, the blood is then returned to the heart via the veinous system.

Oxygen extraction

Fish require oxygen for much the same purpose as terrestrial animals. Extracting it from its dissolved state in the water is carried out through the gills. These organs are found on each side of the head, usually protected by an bony covering called the operculum, or gill cover.

How the gills work

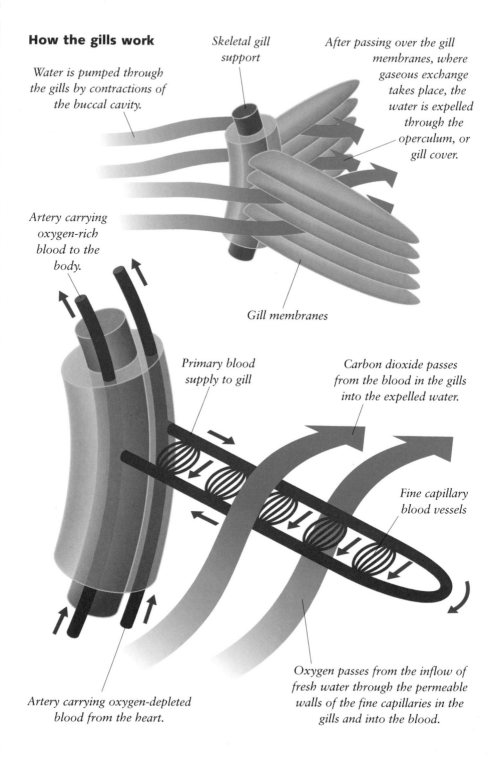

Water is pumped through the gills by contractions of the buccal cavity.

Skeletal gill support

After passing over the gill membranes, where gaseous exchange takes place, the water is expelled through the operculum, or gill cover.

Artery carrying oxygen-rich blood to the body.

Gill membranes

Primary blood supply to gill

Carbon dioxide passes from the blood in the gills into the expelled water.

Fine capillary blood vessels

Artery carrying oxygen-depleted blood from the heart.

Oxygen passes from the inflow of fresh water through the permeable walls of the fine capillaries in the gills and into the blood.

The countercurrent system

To maximize oxygen extraction efficiency, water flows over the gills in the opposite direction to the blood flowing in the capillaries in the gill membranes.

The amount of oxygen in the water is always greater than that in the blood at any particular point. This gradient ensures that the blood continually absorbs oxygen in its passage through the gills.

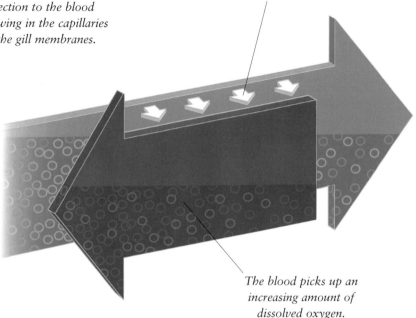

The blood picks up an increasing amount of dissolved oxygen.

Water is first sucked into the mouth. The mouth then closes and the water is pumped back out through the gill opening at the rear of the operculum. The gill filaments are mounted in rows on archlike structures and consist of tiny blood-carrying capillary tubes called lamellae; these give the gills an enormous surface area. Oxygen uptake is further optimized by a counterflow collection system in which blood travels through the gills in the opposite direction to the water flowing over them, thus increasing the time that the blood is exposed to

oxygen-laden water. Additionally, by ensuring that blood is only ever exposed to water with a higher oxygen content than itself, there is never a risk of oxygen diffusing from the blood back into the water. As oxygen is being absorbed into the bloodstream, a simultaneous action also expels carbon dioxide and ammonia from the bloodstream back into the expelled water, with the gills often excreting far more waste than the kidneys.

As dissolved levels of oxygen are usually quite small, the fish has to work hard, even at rest, to maintain a regular supply. In fact, it has been estimated that around 10% of its oxygen consumption is expended just in order to maintain the supply of oxygen in the blood. In some fast-swimming species, the 'open-shut, open-shut' movement sequence of the jaws to keep water moving over the gills is not necessary, as the fish's constant forward movement through the water is enough – as long as the fish remembers to keep its mouth open! Fish that rely on movement for oxygen uptake can suffocate if kept stationary. Fishes in fast-moving waters can also conserve energy during breathing simply by facing into the flow and, again, opening their mouths.

A stickleback's breathing rate is about twice as fast as that of a tench, and sedentary, bottom-dwelling fish generally have a slower respiration rate than fishes that occupy higher levels of the water.

Not all oxygen uptake is achieved by means of the gills. For example, loaches (Cobitidae) can extract oxygen in the hind section of the gut.

Since the oxygen uptake mechanism shares a physical space (at first anyway) with that of food intake – the mouth – you can see that there is an opportunity for conflict. Any solid particles in the water flow would seriously damage the gill filaments, so these are protected by a 'fence' of stiff fibres known as gill rakers that block their passage.

The swimbladder

Any body in water has a finite density, either positive (floating) or negative (sinking), which must be an inconvenience if you wish to change position constantly, moving from one depth to another. How much better if you had an automatic compensating system that took care of things for you, allowing you to remain stationary at any time without the fear of bobbing to the surface or dropping to the bottom.

In fishes, the swimbladder is just such a device. It is an extension of the intestinal canal and lying above it and may be regarded as a hydrostatic organ. As the fish descends, increasing water pressure compresses the organs, making them denser. To re-establish normal density, the swimbladder must inflate. As the fish resurfaces, the expanding swimbladder (under decreasing pressure) needs to be deflated in order to maintain the equilibrium.

The swimbladder may be always open to the rest of the fish's system or may be permanently closed off. In the first instance, the fish makes adjustments of the swimbladder by gulping in air or regurgitating it as required; in the second case, gas is secreted into the swimbladder or absorbed from it through blood capillaries in close contact with the bladder wall.

Not all fishes have swimbladders. Fish with a constantly moving, often high-speed lifestyle, such as sharks, have an enlarged oily liver to give them an 'average' buoyancy. They use their pectoral fins as hydroplanes to alter depth. Bottom-dwelling, more sedentary species, such as gobies, never venture far enough to

How a closed swimbladder works

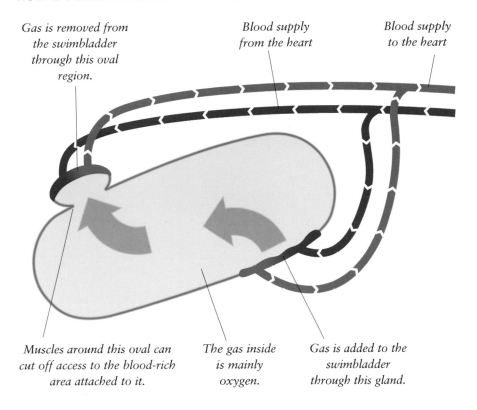

Gas is removed from the swimbladder through this oval region.

Blood supply from the heart

Blood supply to the heart

Muscles around this oval can cut off access to the blood-rich area attached to it.

The gas inside is mainly oxygen.

Gas is added to the swimbladder through this gland.

Left: *As the body shape of cultivated goldfish becomes more egg-shaped, the internal organs become more distorted or compressed. This can impair the efficiency of the swimbladder and lead to swimming balance problems, as here.*

Overleaf: *In common with other bottom-dwelling fishes, this shanny (Blennius pholis) has a less efficient swimbladder because its sedentary lifestyle requires little changes to its overall buoyancy.*

43

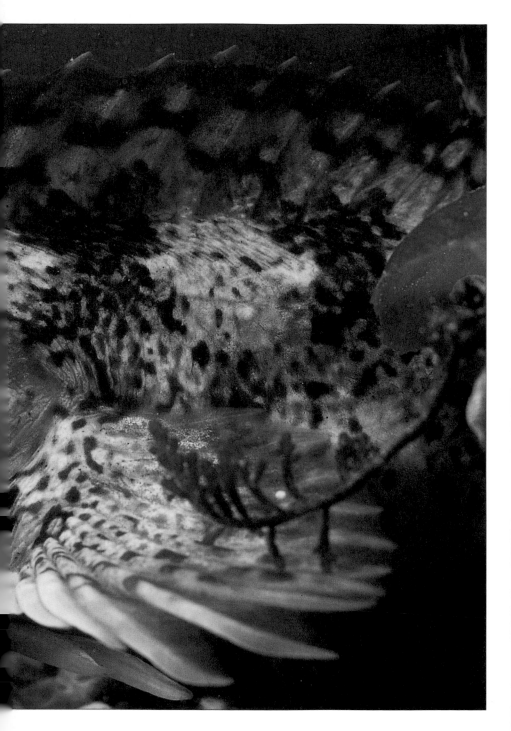

Water regulation in freshwater fish

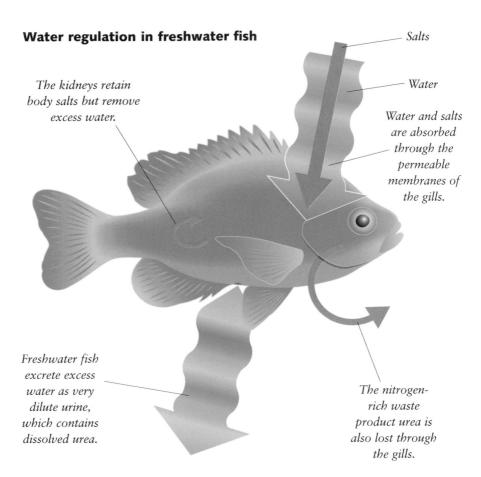

Salts

Water

Water and salts are absorbed through the permeable membranes of the gills.

The kidneys retain body salts but remove excess water.

Freshwater fish excrete excess water as very dilute urine, which contains dissolved urea.

The nitrogen-rich waste product urea is also lost through the gills.

warrant the luxury of a swimbladder.

The function of the swimbladder is not confined to helping fish maintain their position in the water. It can also be used as a resonance chamber, especially in species that produce noises. Similarly, the swimbladder can also act as an amplifier to conduct 'sounds' or vibrations to the inner ear (see page 32).

Osmoregulation

One of the biggest problems for a freshwater fish is the relentless tendency for water to flow into its body. This is due to osmosis, a process in which two liquids of dissimilar densities are separated by a membrane. Translated into 'fish-speak', the two liquids involved are the aquarium water (weak) and the fish's internal body fluids (strong). In osmosis, the natural tendency is for the weaker fluid to move across the membrane (the fish's skin and also gill filaments) to dilute the stronger. This means that the fish is always taking water on board and must rid itself of the surplus to preserve its

Above: Baby eels (elvers) born in salt water face the continuing problem of losing fluid from their bodies to the water around them. They constantly replenish this loss by 'drinking' salt water, excreting the salts and retaining the water.

How long do fishes live?

Fish are different to other living creatures in that they do not grow to a finite size and then stop growing; as long as conditions and food supplies permit, they continue to grow right up to the moment of death. However, the growth rate is not the same throughout their lifetime. In the early years, growth is at its maximum and then gradually decreases. Growth rate is also proportional to seasonal changes, speeding up during warm periods when food is abundant and slowing down as the fish's metabolism slows with decreasing temperatures. Growth (or perhaps more correctly, maturation) does not appear to keep in step between the sexes as, in most instances, the male matures ahead of the female, often by a year or two.

Growth, to final size, is also affected by the size of the water body in which the fish lives. In a lake, for instance, there will be a finite amount of food available and the fish cannot swim away to seek more. If predators are also present then these, too, will take their toll although, paradoxically, the absence of predators allows too

many fish to develop and their growth becomes stunted.

Coldwater fishes grow more slowly, and mature later (in terms of sexual activity) than their relatives in tropical waters. This is because their day lengths are less predictable, temperatures vary, the seasons fluctuate more and the food supply is cut short during the lean winter months. The changes in the seasons, and thus those of growth rate, are reflected in the development of scales with clearly visible annual ridges. Where scales are too small for this to be determined, microscopic examination of the bone cross-sections provides an alternative method of evaluating age.

Typical lifespans of some coldwater fishes (in years)

Stickleback - 3	Koi - 30
Minnows - 3	Plaice - 30
Loaches - 10	Sharks - 30
Pike - 10	Sturgeon - 50
Cod - 20	(or more)
Herring - 20	Catfish - 60
Goldfish - 30	Halibut - 60

normal density. It does this by excreting large volumes of water (up to ten times its own body weight in some instances), but retains any salts in its body to maintain its original fluid strength.

Marine fishes are faced with the same problem but in reverse; because

the surrounding water is stronger than their internal fluid density, they are always losing water, so they must literally 'drink like a fish', excreting very little liquid but plenty of salts.

The phenomenon of 'osmotic pressure' is yet another effect that the fish's metabolism has to contend with and can be one of the stress factors often unwittingly put upon fish when they are transferred between differing water qualities.

How fish strive to stay healthy

We have already discussed the two physical barriers put up by the fish to combat infection and wounds (mucus and scales) but there is also an 'internal' defence system: the immune system. In healthy, well-maintained fish this tides them over the transitional periods of the year when water conditions are liable to vary considerably. Because fish are ectothermic (gain their body heat from outside sources), their body temperature is never very much higher than that of the surrounding water and their metabolic rate varies in sympathy with changes in temperature. During extended cold periods, general activity and bodily functions slow right down. The fish become quite torpid but do not actually hibernate. As temperatures rise in spring, it takes a while before the immune system is restored to its full efficiency, and if water conditions are not at their optimum, the fish will be stressed and less able to deal with any infection.

For example, ammonia is toxic and we have seen that the fish does its utmost to excrete this from the gills. If the filtration system breaks down (or the pond filter has been switched off for the winter), there will be a substantial amount of ammonia (or nitrite) in the water. This can physically affect the structure of the gills, making the absorption of oxygen difficult. In addition, due to the levels of ammonia and nitrite already in the water, the gills may also be prevented from releasing carbon dioxide and ammonia back into the water. Unable to breathe, the fish becomes stressed and overcompensates with adjustments to its vital organs in a attempt to bring relief.

This is only one example of how fish become stressed. Other factors include abrupt temperature changes, transferring from one type of water to another without time to acclimatize, plus the rigours of handling and transportation.

Right: Acipenseridae is one of the longest-living fish families, and contains the sturgeon and sterlet. These fish have body scutes instead of the more conventional scales. They can live for more than 50 years.

SPECIAL ADAPTATIONS

Why are some fish cylindrical whilst others are flat? Why are fish not swept away by water currents? What cunning ways do some fish use to capture their food? How do fish communicate with each other? Here are some answers.

Life in the fast lane

Fast-flowing waters pose problems to fishes wishing to stay in one place. Sheltering behind stones in relatively calm water may be one option.

At first glance, the basic fish shape as discussed on pages 24-49 appears to satisfy all the fish's needs: fins for propulsion and manoeuvring; eyes, nose and mouth for detecting, locating and gathering food; a scale-clad body to aid streamlining and protection, plus very sophisticated systems that allow the fish to position itself effortless at any depth and to build up a picture of its surroundings however turbid the water might be. Yet, if you study fish, there seem to be many deviations from this norm. Why

should this be? The answer is that not all fish inhabit the same type of water and while the 'normal design' is one of compromise, likely to suit most circumstances, extreme conditions require adaptations. These physical adaptations are not limited to where a fish lives, but also reflect what it feeds on. Maintaining its desired position in the water, coupled with the ability to feed efficiently, are certainly two of the most important hurdles a fish needs to clear in order to survive, without even considering self-protection from predators. When you take these factors into account, you can begin to see that the common image of a fish – say, a highly coloured, easily visible goldfish – might have its drawbacks.

Fish that inhabit fast-flowing waters
Let us take fast-flowing waters first. In mountain streams, for example, there is likely to be only a shallow depth of water, but the water will be both clear and well oxygenated. Temperatures may vary quickly but never rise much above 10°C (50°F). Aquatic plant growth may be minimal but, due to the displacement of rocks and boulders, the number of

hiding places and refuges available to the fish may be abundant.

The result is that fishes inhabiting these conditions may not need to adjust to varying depths of water, will not be predated on by large fish and will not have trouble with oxygen-depleted waters. However, without physical modifications to their bodies, they may well live in fear of being swept away by water currents and will find it difficult to collect food with any certainty.

Retaining position is achieved by a combination of physical adaptation and lifestyle. The body of the fish needs to be cylindrical, even vertically compressed, and must certainly have a flattened ventral (lower) surface that presents little resistance to the water flow and prevents the fish being lifted off the bottom by the water flow under its

Left: The hillstream loach (Pseudo-gastromyzon fasciatus) *manages to stay in its chosen resting place by virtue of its pectoral and pelvic fins. These form a suction disk that anchors the fish to the substrate. The flattened ventral surface also prevents water currents getting under the body and sweeping the fish away.*

body. The eel anchors itself by entwining its snakelike body among tree roots or plant stems.

The ventral surface is often 'ruffled' with tiny skin folds to assist friction and the pelvic fins often form partial, or complete, suction pads. The mouth provides the fish with another method of holding on, but this would appear to present a complication if constant breathing is needed. Some species have a special adaptation of the gill chamber that allows 'through-breathing'. Water enters the gill chamber through a vertical slit in the upper part of the chamber, then exits via the gill cover in the normal way. As the fish has to breathe in and out through the same chamber, the respiration rate must be at least double that of the normal 'in-mouth-out of gills' method. Actually, as the intake slit is quite small, respiration rates are often very fast to ensure adequate oxygen uptake. In

this case, breathing bypasses the mouth, leaving it free to act as an anchoring mechanism. Where this facility does not exist, the fishes live a more sedentary life, with less need to move about. This, coupled with freely available oxygen in the water, means that the fish adjusts its breathing rates down to a minimum.

A similar picture emerges in those marine fish that inhabit surf-laden areas of shallow waters. Again, suction-pad modified fins are prominent position-retaining aids, especially in species such as lumpsuckers, clingfishes and gobies.

Another ploy is to make the body as flat as possible, and this is achieved either by compressing the

Below: Flatfishes lie on one side (left or right, depending on species). One eye travels around the body to pair up with the other. Colour patterning varies, too. One side is pale, the other camouflaged.

Above: Cunningly camouflaged by its vertical stripes, the predatory perch (Perca fluviatilis) lies in wait amongst aquatic plants for any passing prey. Its dorsal fin has sharp defensive spines.

body or, in the case of flatfishes, lying on the right or left side. In the latter event, the mouth position has to change obliquely and, even more bizarrely, one of the eyes migrates around the head to take up a new location. This flat-body form is more often found in estuarine fish that take advantage of their flatness to lie within the substrate, further camouflaged by their body colours, which emulate those of their immediate surroundings.

Many fishes that inhabit fast-flowing waters spend their time in the shelter behind or under rocks, only emerging in a quick dash to grab food being swept past them by the water current. These fishes are, therefore, fairly muscularly built and suited for only very short bursts of speed, but they make up for this by having relatively large mouths!

Fish that inhabit slow waters

In slow-moving or stationary waters, where temperatures fluctuate less rapidly and rise to higher values, the fish are able to venture out into the main body of water without fear of being swept away. Their oval-sectioned bodies are often deeper but also laterally compressed, which allows them to hide among aquatic plant stems or in bankside crevices. The perch's vertical dark bandings, for example, disguise its presence very effectively.

However, cylindrical bodies are also in evidence in these conditions, as predatory species also hide amongst plants and sunken tree roots

Above: *The weather loach* (Misgurnus fossilis) *has small eyes, but can locate its food quite easily in muddy waters or at night by feeling for it with a formidable array of barbels equipped with taste buds.*

Below: *The pike's fins are designed to reduce drag and enable it to make sudden bursts of speed. This, together with wide jaws and inward-sloping teeth, allow the fish to make short work of passing prey.*

as they wait to ambush their prey. The pike, with its truncated caudal fin, ideally suited for generating short bursts of speed, has dorsal and anal fins set well back on the body to minimize drag during acceleration in pursuit of a tasty snack. The seahorse has a non-typical body shape. It uses its dorsal fin for propulsion, but anchors itself to any suitable object by using its prehensile tail.

When the water flow is very slow, or even non-existent, the build-up of silt on the substrate is a common occurrence. As the fish forage for food, they stir up the sediment and the resulting cloudy water renders eyesight useless. In this situation, a keen sense of smell and barbels equipped with taste buds are brought into play during the search for food.

Small bodies of stationary water often become devoid of oxygen, and fish living in such circumstances are forced to the surface for air. Cyprinids, such as the carp and the mudminnow *(Umbra krameri)*, gulp in air at the water surface, which is used in the swimbladder. In the mudminnow, the swimbladder is coated with guanin to prevent gases diffusing out. Catfishes and loaches also 'breathe' atmospheric air, using part of their gut to assimilate oxygen and probably remove carbon dioxide from the system.

Defensive strategies

Speed is not everything, so fish must resort to other subterfuges in order 'to eat, but be not eaten.' Any deterrent that prevents a fish being eaten is to be welcomed and a fish's main defences are seen in the form of spines. These are usually found on the dorsal fins, under the eye and on the operculum, or gill cover. Some species are able to erect these spines, not only to prevent themselves being swallowed, but also to lock themselves into crevices to avoid capture. A number of species have poison glands associated with their spines, so these species need particularly careful handling.

Bony plates may also offer some degree of protection against physical damage and it is interesting to note that the number of such plates on the stickleback *(Gasterosteus sp.)* increases in line with the proximity of the fish's habitat to the sea. The horse mackerel *(Trachurus trachurus)* appears to have left nothing to chance in its defensive armoury. It has a second lateral line canal between the first and second dorsal fins, two spines ahead of the anal fin, and the scales of the lateral line have sharp bony edges. Finally, it has an ingenious method of protecting its young. They seek refuge where you would least expect to find them – in the trailing tentacles of jellyfish.

Changing colour has always been a widespread option and, notably, it is the bottom-dwelling species, such as the flatfishes, that are expert at this. Many experiments have been done using species such as plaice to study their reactions when they are laid on backgrounds of varying hues. In most cases, the fish has managed to produce a near match – even when a black-and-white chequerboard background was used! But of course, the flatfishes' usual mode of defence is to burrow into the substrate at the first sign of trouble, leaving perhaps just the high-set eyes protruding.

Chemical communication
Communication between species has to be a sophisticated form of defence, but thanks to fishes' unique sense of smell and taste, subtle chemical changes in the water can be detected and put to good defensive use. When injured, minnows (Phoxinus spp.) give off a fright-substance (a pheromone) that other members of the shoal can detect in time to take evasive action. Similarly, catfish also emit or excrete a communicating substance that provokes or suppresses aggression, depending

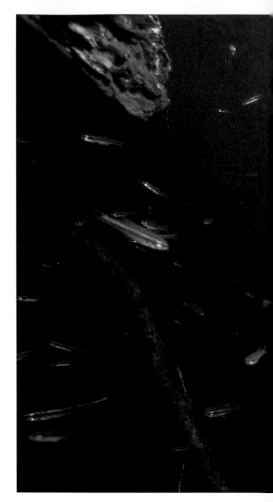

Above: The sight of minnows suddenly fleeing in all directions is a good indication that the release of a fright substance has alerted the shoal to danger from a nearby predator.

Right: The stickleback's defence system consists of a row of sharp spines ahead of the dorsal fin, and bony plates along the body. These make the fish a distasteful meal for any would-be predator.

on circumstance. For example, the North American bullhead *(Ictalurus nebulosus)* is normally a nocturnal species with poor vision but excellent taste and smell senses. When it is in a shoal, it sends out pheromones that not only inhibit aggression but, for instance, supply recipients with information about the size, sex, species and even disposition of other members of the shoal.

Pheromones also play a part in reproduction, acting as a stimulant and as a signal to post-hatched fry. They can govern factors such as development of size or number of fish according to prevailing water conditions, limiting the fish population accordingly. Whereas these effects have been well-documented in tropical fishes, little information appears to be easily available on coldwater subjects, apart from that outlined here.

Feeding adaptations

In the fish world, such is the diversity of foods and methods of collecting them that it is often quite easy to define a species or classify a family within very close limits according to the physical adaptation featured by the fish in its method of feeding.

One early adaptation was the development of protrusible jaws, which work in two ways. Firstly, the jaws and teeth can be brought a little closer to the food source as the fish feeds. Secondly, fish can take advantage of the very nature of the

Left: The tooth-filled jaws of the garpike make escape quite unlikely from the victim's point of view. Once captured, skilful manipulation of the prey makes being swallowed a foregone conclusion.

jaw opening. As the jaws are extended, so a partial vacuum is formed and food is carried into the mouth, along with an inrush of water. The further development of rasping teeth on the outside of the lips also made grazing vegetable matter much simpler, and the intestine in herbivorous fishes is considerably longer than that of carnivorous species.

Similar in its ferocious appearance to the pike, the garpike *(Lepisosteus osseus)* of North America is a fearsome sight, with hugely extended jaws simply bristling with teeth. Observing this species feeding is an object lesson in skill and manipulation. The prey, easily seized by virtue of the fish's speed and gape, is generally captured midbody, crosswise in the jaws. Little by little, the jaws are repeatedly opened and closed so that the prey is rotated to a final position, facing headfirst into the garpike's throat. If the prey fish chooses to make a dash for freedom, it will only end up further down the throat. Only a very brave (and inspired) victim would try to swim out backwards!

A far more genteel approach to feeding is taken by the paddlefish *(Polyodon spathula)*, another North American species. In this instance, just the upper part of the jaw is elongated, forming a flat, spoon-shaped paddle that stirs up the mud on the riverbed. The fish then swims into the resulting cloud of debris to

Above: The sterlet has an upturned snout and a flattened ventral surface, which allow the barbels to seek out food from the substrate most efficiently.

Ideally situated on the very bottom surface of the body and behind the food-locating barbels, the sterlet's mouth acts as a funnel-like extension that allows the fish to suck up food from the substrate.

sift out food particles as water passes through its gaping mouth. Once the food-retaining gill rakers have done their work, the water emerges from the gill openings.

A down-turned mouth, allied to a flattened ventral surface, are natural characteristics of bottom-dwelling species, whose main foods are crustaceans, larvae and worms. The sturgeon and sterlet *(Acipenser* spp.*)* have funnel-shaped mouths that suck up food like a vacuum cleaner from the muddy substrate. Taste-sensitive barbels underneath the tip-tilted snout assist in the detection of food ahead of collection.

Not all fish seek out other living animals to eat; the planktonic species are gentle creatures that merely collect and sieve the surrounding water for microscopic foods. In warm waters there is usually an abundance of plankton, although fish may have to migrate around the seas pursuing its wandering progress. In temperate latitudes, the availability of plankton depends very much on the season; they are only plentiful during the warmer months of the year. To feed on plankton and other tiny foods, fish require some form of straining mechanism in the jaw. The best examples are herring *(Clupea* sp.*)* and the basking shark, *(Cetorhinus* sp.*)* The very large gill rakers of the latter species (often up to 1.25cm/0.5in long) are shed each winter as the food supply wanes.

If you cannot reach your food, the next best thing is to get your food to come to you. The anglerfish *(Lophius* sp.*)* has a special modification to the first of three (separated) rays of its dorsal fin. This terminates in a fleshy appendage that the sedentary anglerfish dangles and twitches over its own mouth in order to attract (and then seize) another fish or other aquatic life form. Some fish round up their food like cowboys. The thresher shark *(Alopias vulpinus)* has a very large upper lobe to the caudal fin with which to thresh the water and drive, or corral, its prey into a group so that it can pick off individuals.

Unnatural changes

All the adaptations described above have evolved naturally in response to the needs of fish and the varying conditions they may encounter. However, in the world of captive fishes it is very much man that plans modifications, and nowhere is this more evident than in the keeping of goldfish and koi. It is the abundance of raw genetic material, especially in the form of the goldfish, that has made all this progress possible (if progress it is).

Over the years, some deviation has been introduced into all areas of the goldfish's appearance. Broader dorsal finnage, trailing caudal fins, and even no fins at all have all been established as desirable features amongst the diverse varieties now available. As well as a wide range of scale forms (see page 26), body shapes, too, have become far removed from the original efficient design. In some cases, these modifications are so extreme that it is doubtful whether a male and female fish could actually swim enough to be able to spawn properly. Indeed, it is likely that many of the more exotic forms are separately hand-stripped of eggs and sperm and never ever meet each other. Nor have the eyes escaped attention. Some fish have up-tilted eyes, while the eyes of others are embellished with fluid-filled sacs below. Curious head-growths and wobbling nasal adornments all bear witness to the fishbreeder's prowess and dedication. Perversely, however, none of these 'improvements' have been shown to benefit the fish at all; as they say, 'beauty is in the eye of the beholder.'

Until relatively recently (considering the fish's long history of cultivation), developments in koi have all been concerned with colour patterning – its definition, intensity and distribution – and its visibility when viewed from above. However, there have been instances of an interest in the development of long-finned varieties (again through selective breeding).

To attract attention in the ever-competitive world of koi-keeping, there have been some examples of koi varieties with differently coloured scales transplanted to other parts of their body, although this appears not to result in a permanent feature. Thankfully, too, the disreputable practice of injecting colour beneath the skin has not followed into the coldwater fish hobby from the tropical fish scene.

Right: Not all adaptations are natural: by using selective breeding techniques, man has added a few of his own.

HOW COLDWATER FISH BREED

The primary function of all animal life is to survive and continue the species. Following courtship and spawning, survival of the eggs is crucial. In some cases, the parent fish actively protect their young during the first few days.

The numbers game

Each of these tiny eggs contains a new fish. By producing millions of these, the survival of many species is ultimately assured.

After a short, temperature-dependent hatching period, young fish are produced from eggs that have been expelled from the female fish and immediately fertilized by the male. With just a few exceptions (generally limited to aftercare of the fertilized eggs), that is all there is to it.

Coldwater fish appear to be not only promiscuous but, in the main, uncaring parents, who are just as likely to eat their own eggs immediately after spawning as not. There is no pair-bonding as with some tropical species, and the act

of reproduction is performed as and when properly conditioned males and females encounter each other. In nature, this action will be seasonal to a certain degree. Usually an increase in daylight hours and water temperature corresponds to an increase in the food supply (insects, small aquatic crustaceans, etc.), which not only ensures that the would-be parent fish are ready to breed, but also that the newly hatched young will have enough food to survive. In the wild, another factor is the influence of a change in water conditions. Late spring brings additional water from melting snow, and the increase in water currents means that the newly fertilized eggs are assured of good aeration, which is essential during the hatching period. The resulting fry will also be dispersed over a wider area.

Differentiating between the sexes
Naturally, each fish must be able to recognize a suitable partner (and the sex of it) before anything constructive can happen. With coldwater fishes, the major clues

to sexual differences are found in coloration, fin shapes and other external signs. With one exception, there is no physical adaptation for fertilization purposes, such as the modification to the anal fin found in male, livebearing tropical species.

Intensification in coloration and/or changes in patterning serve several purposes. Species and sex indication are certainly high on the priority list and the intensification of colour is used by males both to attract females and to deter any rival males. Such are the heightened sensitivities of

Below: When it comes to selecting a mate, competition amongst male sticklebacks is understandably fierce. Those with the best colours and the most determination usually win.

courting males that exposure to a similar colour (regardless of shape or size) may be enough to trigger a retaliatory attack. This can be easily demonstrated using male sticklebacks *(Gasterosteus* sp.), where anything red placed in the tank will be violently assaulted.

While the fish themselves may be perfectly able to sort out the sexes, the fishkeeper often wishes to know them too, in advance of any pre-planned line-breeding programmes.

External visible signs are usually quite easy to see. However, one vitally important piece of external evidence is actually the result of internal changes. Due to the development of eggs within the body at breeding time, the shape of the female when viewed from above takes on a more rounded appearance. This roundness is not always symmetrical and sometimes the female can look decidedly 'lopsided'.

Male cyprinid fishes develop small white pimples (tubercles) on the gill covers. In some species, these may spread over the whole head and on to the rays of the pectoral fins. In some instances, these tubercles look like tiny limpets and you might suppose that these hard growths could cause quite a rasping wound if pressed into offensive/defensive duties. The development of tubercles is not exclusive to male fish; a typical example of both sexes sharing this particular feature is seen in the nase *(Chondrostoma nasus),* a fish found in central Europe.

Other sex-distinguishing features may include bigger or more pointed fins on the male fish and a difference in the size of the vent between the male and female. After all, the female has to pass eggs through her vent, while the male just ejects liquid.

The spawning operation
Eggs (hard roe) are developed in the ovaries of the female fish, while sperm (soft roe) is produced in the testes of the male. It is vital that both eggs and sperm are brought together at the correct moment, and this is at an optimum when both male and female fish are at the peak of condition. At this stage they are described as ripe for breeding.

Once two ripe fish have found each other, the courtship continues and develops into a chase sequence. The male follows the female everywhere, sometimes butting and rubbing against her. (Here, the tubercles may come into arousing play.) Naturally, the female seeks refuge and respite amongst any aquatic plant growth and it is there that the eggs are generally expelled and subsequently fertilized. Most eggs are demersal and slightly sticky, so they sink to the riverbed or lodge in the plants. Any existing water currents may fortuitously take the eggs away from the spawning parents and so deprive them of a tasty snack.

Left to their own devices, the eggs develop over a period of time. Depending on temperature, this may range from a few days to several weeks. The young fish first develops eyes, heart and spinal cord, and shortly after the fins are formed, the tiny fish breaks out of the egg.

Above: One good and reliable guide to sexing cyprinid fishes (here a shiner, Notropis lutrensis) *is that males usually develop small white spots, or tubercles, on the head region at breeding time.*

Variations on a theme

This very 'hit and miss' affair is practised by most members of the Cyprinidae family, including the goldfish, koi, orfe and other ornamental species. In order to ensure quality and optimum survival of the eggs, many fishkeepers seek to control the breeding of their fishes.

During 'courtship', only fishes exhibiting the qualitative features required in the offspring – including coloration, finnage and size – will be allowed to spawn. After spawning is completed, the fishkeeper will take great care to safeguard the fertilized eggs from hungry parent fishes: spawning mats or aquatic plants

Above: The majority of fish eggs are scattered haphazardly and must take their chance of survival by lodging in aquatic plants (or spawning ropes, as here) safe from predators and parents.

laden with eggs will normally be removed from the spawning area to separate hatching quarters.

A further refinement even excludes the two parent fishes from ever meeting each other. Eggs and sperm can be manually stripped from each fish and combined in a bowl to produce fertilized eggs. In commercial breeding stations, the fish can be induced to 'spawn' (provide eggs and sperm) to order practically to the minute, by means of hormone injections.

The Prussian carp *(Carassius auratus gibelio)* adopts a method of reproduction known as parthenogenesis, which means reproduction from an egg without fertilization. Sperm from another male cyprinid fish, such as a common carp or Crucian carp, simply triggers development of the eggs without any genetic fusion taking place, and the resultant fry from these 'unfertilized' eggs are all female.

Just as startling is the existence of hermaphroditic species, in which both male and female organs are not only functionally, but also simultaneously, active. The comber *(Serranus cabrilla)* is able to spawn with another fish of the same species, with both fish acting as male and female at the same time.

Parental care

As we have seen, most coldwater fish follow the same spawning pattern and exhibit no parental care at all, but there are a few notable exceptions, plus one or two extraordinary breeding anomalies.

Some species undertake direct egg and brood protection. The North American Centrarchidae group of fishes, which include the pumpkinseed, excavates shallow, saucer-shaped depressions in the substrate and defends these against intruders during courtship. The eggs are laid, fertilized and subsequently guarded in the same depression.

The stickleback

A well-known nestbuilder is the stickleback. Using aquatic plant materials and algae, the male builds a tunnel-like construction on the substrate and first entices the female to its entrance and then urges her to enter. She lays her eggs within the tunnel and they are fertilized by the male, who then guards the tunnel against allcomers and also encourages water flow through the tunnel by fanning with his fins.

Stickleback spawning behaviour

Left: After the male stickleback has built a tunnel of plant fragments on the substrate, all he has to do is coax the female into it.

Below: Once inside, the female lays eggs, closely watched by the encouraging male.

Right: The male enters the tunnel to fertilize the newly laid eggs. Subsequently, he guards the nest against egg-stealing predators and assists the flow of oxygenated water through the tunnel by fanning with his fins.

Seahorses and pipefishes

The seahorse and the related pipefish have a unique method of caring for their fertilized eggs. The eggs are deposited by the female seahorse into the male's abdominal pouch, where they hatch to produce free-swimming young seahorses. The male pipefish develops folds of skin on its ventral surface within which the fertilized eggs are held until they hatch.

The bitterling

The bitterling *(Rhodeus* spp.*)* has a breeding method that includes a third party in the shape of a freshwater mussel *(Unio* or *Anodonta* spp.*)*

Immediately before spawning, the female fish extends a 5-6cm (2-2.4in)-long tube from her vent. Through this ovipositor she deposits eggs into the mantle area of the mussel via its inhalant siphon. Sperm from the male bitterling is ejected close to the mussel and this, too, is 'inhaled' into the mantle to fertilize the eggs. Subsequently, a continuous supply of water is passed over the developing eggs as the mussel continues to 'breathe'. The young fry are ejected, ready-swimming, at a later date. This safeguarding of its fry is repaid by the fish. Should the

Right: The long ovipositor of the female bitterling is clear to see as she lays her eggs in the inhalant siphon of the mussel. The male's sperm, also ejected near to the siphon, will be drawn in to fertilize the eggs, which can then hatch in safety within the mussel's shell.

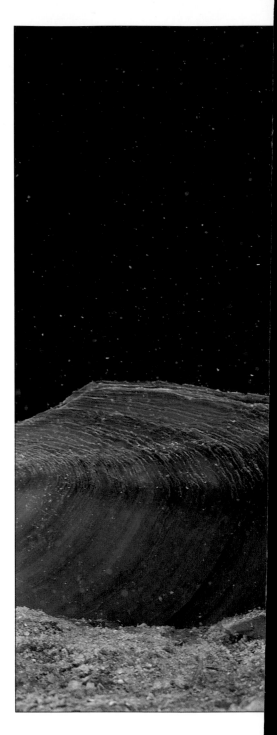

mussel eject some of its own young (known as glochida), they will adhere to the flanks of passing fish and are transported to new locations as these swim along.

The ricefish

An almost subconscious protection of fertilized eggs is practised by the medaka, or ricefish *(Oryzias* sp.*)* Eggs expelled by the female during spawning are not simply scattered haphazardly, but hang like a bunch of miniature grapes from her vent. Eventually, these are brushed off into aquatic vegetation as she swims about, and hatch independently.

Salmon and eels

Two well-known instances of very different spawning procedures occur in coldwater fishes.

The salmon family may well exhibit some egg care by preparing a shallow furrow (called a redd) in the substrate before depositing and fertilizing their eggs, but this factor alone does not set them apart from other fishes. (For example, the grayling, *Thymallus* sp., also creates a nesting area in a depression.)

Salmon spawn in fresh water after spending some considerable time at sea. This means that they must adapt to entirely different conditions twice

Above: Following spawning, the fertilized eggs of the medaka (Oryzias sp.) hang like a bunch of grapes from the female's vent before being brushed off into the aquatic plants as she swims around. There they subsequently hatch.

Right: Having adapted to fresh water from sea water, the salmon battles upstream, surviving waterfalls and predators, to reach calmer waters, where its eggs will be laid and fertilized. Very few parent fish survive once spawning is completed.

Below: Salmon return to the same river in which they were born. It is thought that they relocate their 'birth-river' by smell or taste.

during their lifespan: once as they migrate to the sea after growing up in the fresh waters of their spawning ground and then, as they return from the sea to the same waters in which they began their lives, they must recondition themselves to fresh water. The final adaptation is terminal, as most adult salmon die after spawning. However, the sturgeon's spawning does not end on such a tragic note, for after re-entering fresh water to spawn, the adult fish return to the sea.

This scenario is reversed in eels (*Anguilla* spp.), which live for many years in fresh water before returning to the sea to spawn. Adult eels also die after spawning and it is at least a year or so before the fry eventually make their way back to the continental shelf. They then re-enter freshwater rivers, where they mature over several years before making their final trip back to the sea to spawn and continue the species.

Below: The eel spends several years in fresh water before descending to the sea, where it travels to the Sargasso Sea to spawn. The process of migration from fresh to salt water is called catadromy.

Right: In springtime, thousands of silver elvers – young eels – make their way into estuaries and rivers to develop into adults. They often travel overland during damp, dewy nights.

KEEPING COLDWATER FISH

There are many things to consider when keeping coldwater fish. Should you choose native or cultivated species? Should they be housed in an aquarium or pond, and what fish are best suited to either – or can any fish be kept in both?

Setting aside for the moment the question of size of fish, the one consideration that could influence the choice between setting up a pond or aquarium for coldwater fish must be colour. However beautifully you landscape your pond and however attractive the waterfalls and cascades, the feature that completes the picture – the fish – will be completely wasted if they are invisible due to their dull colours. However, unless you have sufficient space to house commodious aquariums, then a pond has to be the

Vibrant pond fishes

Bold red and white markings and long fins make these sarasa comets highly visible and decorative additions to the outdoor pond.

place for the larger species, regardless of their coloration. Having said that, it is important to realize that not all highly coloured, easily seen fish will be able to tolerate all-year-round accommodation in an outside pond!

The advantages of a pond are many: it adds other dimensions to the garden, such as the sound of moving water and the arrival of colourful insects and amphibians. It can be combined with that other popular pastime, gardening, and there is no limit to the number of hours you can be (apparently) busy, pottering around the water's edge. Finally, and this is even before we consider the fish, it gets you out into the fresh air.

On the other hand, the aquarium is indeed an all-year-round activity and you are (theoretically, at least) in complete control of its conditions. There is an added bonus here, too; unlike the pond, which can only be viewed from above, with an aquarium you can see the fish from all sides. You can study their lifestyle and, if necessary, tailor the water conditions to suit each species' requirements. In addition, although you will be 'house-bound', there will be no ice problems or predators to contend with.

On the following pages we outline basic pond and aquarium care. There is much information that is relevant to both so, to avoid unnecessary duplication, it is a good idea to read both sections, regardless of where your actual fishkeeping activities lie.

The basic pond

While the overall size of any pond will be dictated by the proportions of your garden and the available space, there is one important parameter that remains constant whatever the area of water: depth.

In order to maintain reasonably stable conditions throughout the year, any pond should have a minimum average water depth of 45cm (18in), with a section reaching down to 60 or even 75cm (24-30in). This will be suitable for most coldwater fish, including goldfish. Ponds with a surface area of 3.5m^2 (38ft^2) or less are generally unsatisfactory from the aesthetic point of view and the chances of fishkeeping success are reduced. However, if you wish to keep koi, you should increase the maximum water depth to about 150cm (60in) to enable the fish to develop fully. It is important to realize that, in general, to balance this greater depth, koi ponds are much larger than the

Pond stocking levels

Unlike the indoor aquarium, where the total fish-holding capacity can be calculated fairly accurately, the pond's potential fish-holding capacity often seems incalculable, if only because it is difficult to measure its surface area and/or volume. An accepted guide for a new pond is to allow 25cm (10in) of fish for every 1m^2 (10ft^2) of water surface area. In an established pond, where the filtration system is fully matured and operating at maximum efficiency, this allowance may be doubled, i.e. 50cm (20in) for every 1m^2 of surface area. Both these stocking levels allow for growth. Suitable pond fish are discussed in the section on pages 96-123.

Left: Colourful koi show up well against the dark bottom of the pond. An oriental-style pergola and pondside decorations complete the scene.

average garden pond housing a range of goldfish and smaller pond fish.

Water temperatures in shallow ponds vary rapidly, overheating in summer and cooling down too quickly in winter. Water loss through evaporation, freezing solid in winter and rampant algae growth in summer are frequent problems.

Siting the pond

Assuming that the pond is to accommodate both fish and aquatic plants, it is important that it receives direct sunshine for most of the day, particularly if you wish to include flowering waterlilies. Additionally, the pond should be sited well away from deciduous, shade-giving trees, whose adventitious roots may cause damage to the pond structure and whose leaves will fill the pond in autumn and cause pollution.

Lining materials

A preformed pond made from glass-reinforced plastic (GRP) should have marginal shelves moulded into its design for the planting of shallow water aquatic plants. With preformed ponds you will be limited to what the manufacturer feels is the ideal shape, size and colour; always remember that a preformed pond looks larger when out of the ground.

Planning your own pond by digging a free-formed hole and lining it with a good-quality lining material such as butyl rubber is the most popular option. Whatever your choice of materials, mark out the shape of the pond in your garden with a length of rope or a hosepipe and make adjustments to the size and shape before you start digging or, especially, ordering lining materials.

Koi ponds are usually built from aerated concrete blocks covered with a rendering coat of cement and then sealed to prevent lime leaching out into the water.

Filtration systems

Providing and maintaining good water quality is essential. Although the pond may well be 'self-cleaning' to a degree through the action of the wind and rain, it is important that toxic ammonia-based compounds are removed from the water. A suitable biological filter, in which nitrifying bacteria will convert ammonia to nitrite and then nitrate, can be located either in the pond, sunk in the ground alongside or set in a rockery. This final option is very popular, as the water returning from the filter can be directed back to the pond via a waterfall or cascade. A submersible pump placed in the pond pumps water to the filter. Such a pump may also be supplied with an optional fountain jet, although such pumps may not be capable of adequately delivering solid waste material to the filter. A separate 'solids-handling' pump is best for the filtration system.

A filtration system such as this would be suitable for a typical goldfish pond, but there is a complication with a koi pond. Koi have voracious appetites that include a taste for aquatic plants, so plants

Below: As you fill the pond with water, smooth the liner into place and then trim the edge. The 'step' left around the excavation of this lined pond provides a shelf on which paving stones can be laid.

Typical pond filter system

UV unit

Reinforced wide diameter hose concealed in the rockery.

Above: *Water from the pond reaches the UV lamp, first through the as yet unburied, or otherwise hidden hose before passing through the filter chambers and returning to the pond via a cascade.*

The filter unit should contain suitable media to provide mechanical and biological filtration.

Place a submersible pump in the pond. A pump capable of passing solids is best.

are not generally included in a koi pond. Koi also produce a great deal of waste. As the water has lost one of its natural 'cleaners' – plants – you will have to make up the loss by installing a much bigger filtration system. As a rough guide, the volume of the filter unit should be about one-third that of the main pond.

A koi pond also has a great deal of water engineering associated with it. A drainage system is usually installed before the main pond is built to draw water from the bottom of the pond. Additional feeds to the filtration system (usually installed in the ground alongside the main pond) are generally made directly through the side walls of the pond. The filtered water is then pumped back to the pond by a pump situated after the filtration unit. Fortunately, koi pond designers are very adept at disguising the filtration unit. It can be covered with wooden decking to provide an excellent, and decorative, pondside viewing position.

Biological filtration

While any filtration unit should be capable of straining suspended visible matter from the water, the real job is done by the biological section. To ensure good filtration, this section must be allowed to 'mature' over a long period (often weeks). You will find details of fish stocking levels and how to calculate them on page 77, but on no account should you add the total number of fish to the pond

Left: Koi ponds require very efficient filtration systems to keep water quality at optimum conditions. Filters are usually sited alongside the main pond, but they can be hidden under decorative decking. This is easy to remove for regular and necessary maintenance.

Planting a waterlily

1 The leaves of a newly planted waterlily may not be able to float on the water surface. Use a clean, upturned plastic pot to raise the lily up to the correct height. A black pot is less visible.

2 To wash surplus soil from the basket, make sure that the lily is thoroughly watered before placing it in the pond. Add a generous layer of gravel to the surface to stop fish digging out the soil.

at once. Add fish gradually over a long period, so that the bacteria in the filter can keep in step with the work load. If you intend to switch off the filtration unit during the winter, remember that it will need time to mature again the following spring. If there is a large number of fish in the pond in early spring, some could be at risk from any excess ammonia and nitrite in the water.

Planting up a pond

Aquatic plants play a valuable role in the pond as water purifiers, but in a well-designed garden pond they take on a decorative role, too. There are pond plants to suit every location in the pond; some live in deep water, others thrive in shallow water on the marginal shelves, while others will flourish in damp soil around the edge of the pond.

Aquatic plants range from tiny, free-floating mosses and the so-called 'oxygenators' to the exquisite waterlilies. Marginal plants range from irises to stately arum lilies by way of rushes and scarlet lobelias.

The greatest service provided by the plants is to compete against troublesome green algae for nutrients in the water. These nutrients usually build up because the fishkeeper neglects to remove dead and decaying vegetation from the pond in the autumn. The following spring, usually well ahead of long periods of

Keeping non-cultivated fishes

Right from childhood, many people have kept fishes, usually beginning with 'tiddlers' triumphantly brought home in a jar from the local park lake or nearby stream.

Today, the situation is more limited. With an eye to conserving and protecting native stocks, legislation has been brought in to control the movements of species that may be endangered in their own right or that may endanger existing fauna if they are introduced into local waterways. To this end, anyone wishing to stock fish for future sale or buy them needs to obtain the necessary licences.

There have always been local laws that determine what may, or may not, be removed from the wild. (Members of angling societies will be well acquainted with these.) In some areas, there are similar restrictions on the movements of amphibians, such as newts.

It is vital that no captive fishes are ever released into the wild, especially those from countries that share the same climatic conditions. Such fishes may not only thrive in local waters, but may well introduce disease, decimate (or even hybridize with) local stocks and transform the whole aquatic population.

Be sure to check your local regulations if you are in any doubt. These will vary from country to country and from state to state.

sunshine that otherwise stimulate the growth of the desirable aquatic plants, algae take full advantage of the food available and rapidly turn the pond water green. Fortunately, incorporating an ultraviolet lamp into the filter system clears up this problem within a few weeks. Once a proportion of the pond surface is covered with the large floating leaves of a waterlily, their shade cuts down the amount of light entering the pond (a contributing factor to the growth of filamentous algae called blanketweed) and the pond finds its own natural balance, or equilibrium.

To retain control of their rampant growth, grow aquatic plants in planting baskets. It makes the job of repositioning and/or maintaining the plants much easier. Cover the top of the soil in the baskets with a layer of gravel or pebbles to prevent foraging fish from digging out the soil and muddying the pond water. Place baskets containing young waterlilies that have yet to reach their mature stem length on a pile of bricks (or an upturned bucket) so that their leaves float on the surface; lower them into deeper water as they grow.

Oxygenating plants are fast-growing, free-floating species that literally 'add' oxygen to the water during daylight hours. (You can see the bubbles appearing on the leaves.)

They also provide suitable spawning material in which the fish can lay their eggs. Paradoxically, too many oxygenating plants can cause oxygen deficiency during hot summer nights. The plants give off carbon dioxide which, combined with low oxygen levels in the warm water, will cause the fish to gasp at the water surface. Thin out oxygenators as a matter of course during the summer; they make good garden compost!

Feeding pond fish

With fish in an aquarium you can see immediately whether they are feeding properly or merely mouthing at it and spitting it out. Depending on the type of food offered, this may not be quite so easy in a garden pond. Again, aquarium fish are only fed at their owner's convenience, whereas in the pond there is plenty of natural food available from spring until autumn and any added by the fishkeeper may

well be superfluous to requirements. Because of the unknown quantities of natural food available in the pond, it is important not to overfeed with prepared foods. Using floating types will allow you to gauge just how quickly it is being eaten (or not), but do not forget to add some fast-sinking foods for any bottom-dwelling fish you may have.

Feeding pond fish provides you with an excellent opportunity to check the fish population. Do look for any absentees, as their dead bodies could well be polluting the pond water. Be wary of giving aquatic live foods collected from fish-carrying waters, as they may be carriers of disease.

Below: Oxygenating plants, such as this hornwort (Ceratophyllum sp.), need not be planted but can be left floating in the pond. Fish (and amphibians) make use of them as spawning media.

85

The basic aquarium

In order to maintain optimum, stable water conditions and accommodate what can be sizable fish (when compared to their smaller tropical relatives), a coldwater fish aquarium should measure at least 90cm long by 30cm front to back and up to 38cm deep (36x12x15in). This will afford a reasonable surface area for oxygen absorption and provide adequate swimming space.

When considering which coldwater fish to include in the aquarium, bear in mind that native (non-cultivated) fishes require very well-oxygenated, well-filtered water, together with ample swimming space for growth. The same can be said for koi, but you should be prepared for very rapid growth under such ideal conditions, especially as the water temperatures are likely to be consistently above those found in the outside pond. When transferring aquarium-kept koi to an outside pond, try to avoid thermal shock by carrying out the operation when the two water temperatures are the same.

Filtration for aquariums

Most coldwater fish are energetic and active, and require a good supply of both food and oxygen. An excellent filtration system will take care of the oxygenation, but the fishkeeper must deal with the ammonia waste.

In this instance, it is a good idea to use a combination of filtration units. Place an internal power filter at each end of the aquarium to draw water through a filter sponge medium and re-release it back into

the aquarium under pressure. Often, this is done via an air intake or venturi to add extra air to the water.

Alternatively (if, say, there is a convenient space below the aquarium), use a large external canister-type power filter that does not cut down on the fishes' swimming space, as is the case with internal models. In this event, fit double taps in the 'flow' and 'return' tubes to the external filter to

Above: Internal power filters can be placed in a rear corner of the tank. Use one unit in each corner in large tanks. As well as cleaning the water, they create circulating currents to aid oxygenation.

An aquarium with an external power filter

External power filters can be sited below the aquarium, concealed in a wooden cabinet. Two isolating taps (immediately above the filter canister) shut off the water flow so that the filter unit can be removed for cleaning. With the inlet and outlet hoses at opposite ends of the tank, a waterflow is created through the aquarium.

Place the intake assembly in a rear corner of the tank, with the strainer basket just above the substrate.

Position the return jet in the other rear corner so that the flow is at, or just above or just below, the water surface. Attach it to the outside glass with the suckers provided.

Use a sheet of polystyrene or plastic foam as cushioning between the all-glass tank and the stand or cabinet.

Power canister filters vary in design, but not in principle. Water is drawn through various media that remove dirt particles and break down harmful organic waste. The cleaned water is then returned to the tank.

facilitate maintenance. Turning off the taps isolates the aquarium from the filter, which can then be removed for cleaning. Filling the filter with water, reconnecting and turning on the taps eliminates the need to reprime the filter.

Biological filtration can be carried out by the usual (although increasingly outdated) undergravel system. Lay a plastic mesh fitted with airlift tubes on the base of the aquarium before adding the substrate material. There should be at least 5cm (2in) of substrate material above the filter mesh and a secondary plastic mesh should be fitted at the 'half-depth' point. This protects the filter plate from being exposed (and

Below: Lighting in this hinge-supported hood is protected against damage from water splashes or condensation by a waterproof cover. The starter unit is concealed behind a separate panel.

thus 'short-circuited') by digging, foraging fishes.

Water is drawn through the system by electric powerheads fitted to the top of each uplift tube. Recently developed 'fluidized bed' designs also use bacterial activity in an external unit containing a gravel-type medium through which water is pumped. To maintain water conditions, carry out a partial water change (about 20%) every month.

Lighting

An indoor aquarium is generally best sited away from direct sunlight. In this way, you can exercise complete control over the lighting and discourage unwanted algae growth. Another advantage is that, because the aquarium is out of the sunlight, water temperatures will not rise unduly during summer months.

If you propose to include aquatic plants in the aquarium, you must

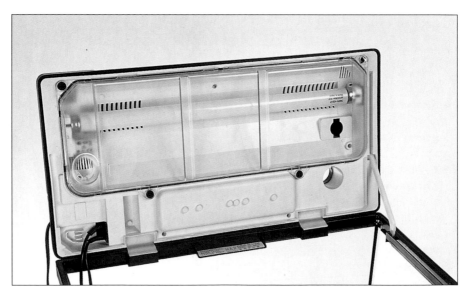

Left: The 'safe zone' shown on this tropical aquarium thermometer can be regarded as a danger zone for coldwater fish. Check the temperature regularly, particularly during spells of hot weather, and cool the water down if necessary.

Temperature

The water temperature within a 'coldwater' aquarium will fluctuate naturally according to ambient temperatures. Generally, these changing temperatures will not inconvenience the fishes, except in the middle of summer. At this time, they may rise to uncomfortable limits and reduce oxygen levels in the aquarium, especially if it receives direct sunlight. If this happens, provide extra aeration (and tank shading if necessary), perhaps coupled with a partial water change using cooler water. Alternatively, floating a bag of ice-cubes in the tank will help. If summer temperatures are likely to be consistently high, it may be worth investing in a chiller

provide sufficient light to stimulate their growth. Use two 30 watt fluorescent tubes to illuminate the tank for 8-10 hours a day, but trial and error will show what periods of illumination give the best results. Mercury vapour lamps are excellent for supporting plant growth in tanks.

Tank stocking levels

As the aquarium is to be a strictly controlled environment, it is possible to make a calculation to determine a maximum total body length of fishes. In this instance, allow 2.5cm (1in) of fish length (not including the tail) per 150cm² (24in²) of surface area. Thus an aquarium measuring 90x30x38cm (36x12x15in) has a surface area of 90x30cm = 2,700cm² (432in²) and is theoretically capable of holding a maximum of 45cm (18in) of fish. In practical terms, this means that the aquarium will accommodate, say, five 9cm (3.5in) fishes but, as in the pond example, this total should be built up over a period of time. Do not add all the fish to the aquarium at once, as the filter will not be able to cope with the sudden increase in waste materials.

Using plastic plants in the aquarium

Limnophila aquatica
*(formerly called
ambulia)*

Ceratopsis cornuta
(Indian fern)

Myriophyllum

1 Plastic plants are easy to position in the aquarium. Simply hold the plant at the base and push it firmly into the substrate so that it cannot be seen.

2 Fill the clear plastic trough at the base with gravel to prevent the plant floating. You can position plastic plants before filling the tank with water.

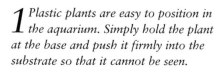

Above: *Plastic plants offer shelter and spawning sites but do not play any role in oxygenating or otherwise purifying the water. Position larger plants at the back and sides of the tank and keep smaller examples in the foreground.*

A selection of prepared aquarium foods

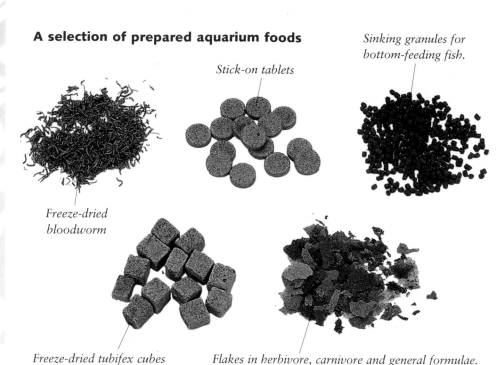

Stick-on tablets

Sinking granules for bottom-feeding fish.

Freeze-dried bloodworm

Freeze-dried tubifex cubes

Flakes in herbivore, carnivore and general formulae.

Left: *Live foods, such as these water fleas (Daphnia sp.), are useful for bringing fish into breeding condition. If in doubt as to their cleanliness, use frozen or freeze-dried supplies. Avoid live tubifex worms, as they inhabit polluted mud.*

Right: *Bloodworms, along with other waterborne insect larval forms, make a refreshing and nutritious change from prepared dried foods. Frozen and freeze-dried forms of these foods are available.*

system. Often, standing the external power filter canister in an ice-filled bucket will help to bring down the aquarium water temperature.

Planting the aquarium

Tall, grassy types of plant, such as *Vallisneria* and *Sagittaria*, can be planted to good effect around the back and sides of the aquarium. Bushy species, such as *Myriophyllum* and *Elodea* are fast growers from which cuttings can be replanted to form extra plant stock. It may be worth placing some large pebbles on the substrate around the bases of plants to prevent them being

Below: Use tall, grasslike plants, such as vallisneria (shown here) and sagittaria, to mask the back and side glass 'walls' of the aquarium.

uprooted by the fish. If you plan to keep large fish (in a suitably sized tank) furnish the aquarium with plastic replica plants. In this case, you can decrease the amount of light, as artificial plants will not photosynthesize as the real ones do. Should they become overgrown with algae you can remove them and scrub them clean.

Feeding aquarium fish

Many aquarium problems can be attributed to overfeeding. It is important that the fish actually eat all you give them within a few minutes. Any excess food should be removed. It is likely that you will be feeding one of the many quality prepared foods available on the market. Try to vary the brands, so that your fish do not become accustomed to one type of food.

It is possible to offer fish live 'aquatic' foods, such as daphnia (water fleas) and bloodworms. If these are collected from the wild, do make sure they are obtained from disease-free sources. Your aquatic dealer will usually have good quality, reliable live foods in stock, together with their equally nutritious freeze-dried or frozen equivalents.

Many garden insects and bugs also make excellent fish food. Aphids and caterpillars are relished, as are gnat larvae from rain-butts. 'Non-polluted' garden worms are fine.

Overleaf: Fish use oxygenating plants, such as this Elodea canadensis, *as spawning sites and also find supplies of microscopic live foods amongst them.*

A SELECTION OF COLDWATER FISH

Is there a large range of coldwater fish available and, if so, which are the most popular? Are some more appropriate for the pond than the aquarium? Are there any totally unsuitable fish that ought to be left alone?

Goldfish or koi are usually the first choice, the deciding factor being space. Goldfish may be kept in an aquarium or pond, although certain fancy varieties may not be entirely suitable for ponds throughout the year. Larger fish, such as koi and orfe, are best seen in outdoor ponds.

Carassius auratus – *Goldfish*

The goldfish is the universal 'aquatic workhorse' and the world's most widely kept fish. Thanks to years of intensive and selective breeding programmes, it is available in a multitude of forms and colours.

Goldfish can be divided into two basic groups: singletails and twintails, both of which can have three different scale types, namely metallic, nacreous and matt. Added to these characteristics are different body shapes and fin patterns.

Varieties from the singletail group – common goldfish, London and Bristol shubunkins and comets – are best suited to outdoor ponds. They

Below: These goldfish are classed as 'singletails', their caudal fins being a simple, single, forked fin. They are suitable for all-year-round pond life.

are hardy, can overwinter (even beneath ice) and their excellent swimming capabilities mean they can compete for food and probably outrun the fishkeeper's net with ease.

Twintail varieties, with more exaggerated finnage and egg-shaped bodies, would benefit by being considered aquarium subjects. They are less hardy and need cosseting from the rigours of winter and dirty pond water. However, the fantail, although a twintail, may just creep into the 'pond-suitable' category.

After a hectic chase through aquatic plants or spawning brushes, breeding follows the typical egg-scattering pattern.

Below: It is not its many colours that identify this London shubunkin, but the shape and size of its caudal fin.

Right: This Bristol shubunkin variety differs from other shubunkins in that the caudal fin is much larger and has rounded lobes. Ideally, these should not overlap in a scissorlike fashion.

Above: The red area on the back of this fantail – a twintail variety – not only gives it a smart look, but also makes it easier to see in a pond. The divided caudal fin should always be held stiffly.

Below: Close examination of the scales of this pearlscale variety reveals that each scale has a white domed centre, giving it a raised appearance. The body is often quite well rounded.

Below: *The comet goldfish has exaggerated fin lengths, including the pectoral, pelvic and caudal fins. The caudal fin is almost as long as the body* of the fish itself. Comets are capable of very fast swimming speeds, but only over short distances. Even so, this is enough to make netting them extremely difficult.

Above: Orandas show several developments: egg-shaped bodies, twin tails and divided anal fins. They also have the decorative raspberry-like growth (known as the 'wen') over the head.

Left: These ranchu, the Japanese equivalent of the lionhead variety, have severely turned-down caudal peduncles and lack the dorsal fin.

Above: *The celestial also lacks a dorsal fin, but its development centres on the eyes, which, as a result of selective breeding, have become trained to gaze everlastingly in an upward direction.*

Left: *The bubble-eye could not have a more descriptive name. The fluid-filled sacs beneath each eye are very delicate, which limits this fish to aquarium life only.*

Cyprinus carpio – Koi

Although small koi can be kept in a suitably sized aquarium, they are generally considered to be pond fish, and their development through the years has always been with this intention in mind. Their colourful markings have been deliberately arranged on the body (through selective breeding programmes) to be viewed from above, against the dark background of the pond's depths.

Koi require special care, particularly with regard to the design of their pond. As well as plenty of swimming space, water depth is an important factor, as is attention to maintaining water quality. Unfortunately, the koi's voracious appetite means that it produces correspondingly large quantities of waste, so an efficient filtration system is essential. Such a system must be planned and incorporated when the koi pond is installed; converting an existing goldfish pond is not always a practicable proposition.

Bear in mind that seasonal transitions – winter to spring and summer to autumn – are critical stages in the care of koi. Their dietary needs also alter at these times. Paying careful attention to preparing koi for the winter and monitoring their subsequent emergence in spring will pay dividends and help to keep them in excellent condition, both in health and in appearance.

Above: Koi are constantly on the move around the pond. Here they appreciate the flow of well-oxygenated water as it returns to their pond down a cascade.

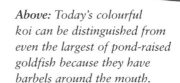

Above: Today's colourful koi can be distinguished from even the largest of pond-raised goldfish because they have barbels around the mouth.

Above: It is not until you see koi against a dark pond background that you realise how skilfully their colour patterns have been developed to be shown to best advantage.

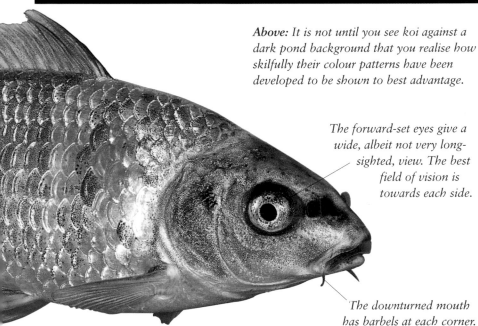

The forward-set eyes give a wide, albeit not very long-sighted, view. The best field of vision is towards each side.

The downturned mouth has barbels at each corner.

103

Above: The dark-centred scales on this koi are reminiscent of a pinecone. This effect is called Matsuba. The dark scale centres should be clearly defined. Non-metallic coloured koi are classified in the Kawarimono class.

Above: This single-coloured, metallic-scaled variety of koi is known as an Ogon. Its classification, for exhibition purposes, is Hikari Muji-mono. Although traditionally gold, silver is also popular.

Right: Although this is a koi, it might not conform to today's recognized patternings. At best, while it shows startling blue coloration and a well-defined lateral line, it might be described as a brocaded carp.

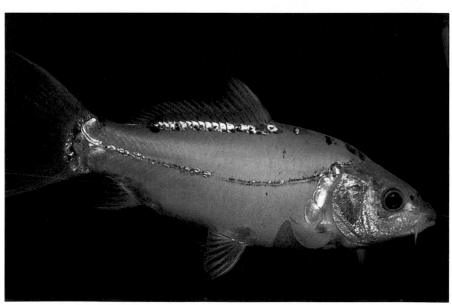

Orfe and other cyprinids

The orfe *(Idus idus)* is a slim, streamlined fish that loves to cruise in the upper levels of the water. In summer it often leaps out of the water (whether from natural exuberance or in pursuit of insects), so pondkeepers with small ponds should not be surprised to find an orfe on the lawn! Naturally, the cultivated gold and blue forms are more visible than the drab, olive-green wild form. Orfe are especially susceptible to oxygen depletion and are usually the first to succumb following warm, thundery weather. Keep fountains and waterfalls running during such times.

The tench *(Tinca tinca)* is another species whose cultivated gold form shows up better in the pond than the natural species. However, being a bottom-dweller, even the gold coloration can be hard to see.

If it is to breed, the bitterling *(Rhodeus amarus)* will need to be accompanied in the pond by a freshwater mussel. It may be preferable to house both in an aquarium so that you can watch the

Below The golden orfe is the popular ornamental form of a silver fish. It cruises endlessly in the upper waters of the pond and loves the sunshine. It is very susceptible to oxygen depletion.

Right: In addition to having a unique breeding method, the bitterling also possesses colours that, under certain lighting conditions, can rival anything a 'tropical' species might display.

Left: *The orfe has not escaped man's desire to tinker genetically, and this blue form is yet another example. A red and white form has also been produced. Orfe are expert at jumping out of the pond.*

fascinating breeding technique in detail (see page 70). Similarly, the tunnel-building activity of the stickleback *(Gasterosteus aculeatus)* during spawning (described on page 68) would pass unnoticed in a pond.

The pale chub *(Zacco platypus)* from China and Japan is one coldwater fish whose finnage may be adapted for spawning. The male's anal fin is much extended, and as well as being a useful aid in distinguishing the sexes, it may also play an important role in fertilizing eggs by channelling the sperm towards the female's vent as eggs are expelled from her body.

The dace, shiner and members of the minnow group are probably too small to be seen and enjoyed in a pond. As their colours are best viewed from the side, it would be better to keep these fish, too, in a well-aerated aquarium.

Above: Minnows, one of the most popular 'tiddlers' of everyone's childhood, require well-oxygenated water to survive in captivity. Keep them in a small shoal.

Below: The stickleback, the hunting of which formed the most popular of childhood pastimes, has a very sophisticated breeding behaviour.

Above: The pale chub (Zacco platypus) is brilliantly marked with vertical bands of blue. The large anal fin of the male is presumed to be a spawning aid.

Below: It is a pity that the very smart-looking appearance of Sarcocheilichthys sinensis *is slightly undermined by its popular name of oily gudgeon.*

*Right: The clicker barb
(Pseudorasbora parva)
has dark rear edges to
its grey scales, which
give the fish a netted
appearance. This fish
develops breeding
tubercles on the head
at spawning time. First
found in the Far East,
it now inhabits waters
of central Europe.*

Left: The southern redbelly dace (Phoxinus erythrogaster) *from North America is a colourful fish with iridescent flanks. At spawning time, males may have head tubercles and yellow or bright red bellies. To see the males at their most colourful, keep them in a shoal containing both sexes.*

Above: *The central mudminnow (Umbra limi) has one or two survival tricks up its sleeve. It can utilize atmospheric air and is also said to lie dormant in the mud during adverse conditions.*

Below: *The shiner (Notropis lutrensis) is another coldwater fish with colours to rival those of tropical species. The red and purple hues are intensified dramatically during spawning.*

Below: The fathead minnow (Pimephales promelas) *has two forms: the natural form is greenish silver, but this golden form has been popular with fishkeepers for many years. It does well in ponds and aquariums. Its common name is derived from the blunt and stocky appearance of the adult's head.*

Right: This is the fishkeeper's answer to those wanting to keep a visible tench – the golden form. The flattened ventral surface is a clear indication that this is a bottom-dwelling fish, a fact borne out by pond owners who rediscover their tench when clearing silt from the pond bottom.

Below: The lateral line system is clearly visible on the flanks of this normal-coloured tench (Tinca tinca). Its body is also covered in a thick mucus reputed to have a healing effect on ailing fish that rub themselves against this 'doctor fish'. Male tench have longer pelvic fins.

Sunfishes – Centrarchidae

Sunfishes, and the related basses, are popular with anglers in their native North American waters, such is the spirited fight they offer when caught. However, one or two are quite brightly marked and make excellent aquarium subjects. A useful aid to positive identification of sunfish species is often the size or shape of the earlike extension to the upper part of the gill cover. The spawning habits of most sunfishes are also a source of interest: some build shallow depressions in the substrate in which to spawn; in others, males undergo a startling colour change, in one instance from drab grey to black.

Right: The black-banded sunfish (Enneacanthus chaetodon) is a small North American species whose brilliant orange and black markings are intensely displayed at breeding time and best seen in the aquarium.

Left: The pumpkinseed (Lepomis gibbosus), *one of the sunfishes, is a popular sporting fish with anglers, but as it is not too large, it is also a popular choice for a pond or the larger aquarium. Its blue-green markings are especially attractive when seen under side-lighting conditions. The 'ear' is marked with a red edge.*

Other genera

The top and bottom levels of the pond or aquarium are home to many fishes. One of the most intriguing top-swimmers is the medaka, or ricefish *(Oryzias latipes)*. A golden form is popular with fishkeepers as it has an interesting spawning habit: after spawning, the fertilized eggs remain attached to the female's vent for some days. The ricefish can also survive quite low temperatures and can be kept outside in ponds, even under ice.

Species living on the riverbed often lack a swimbladder due to their limited range of movements. The loaches are thickened, wormlike fish, with an erectile spine below the eye.

Below: The weather loach (Misgurnus anguillicaudatus) *is so-named because it becomes restless as barometric pressure falls, indicating the approach of stormy weather. Young weather loaches often leave the water for short periods.*

They are, to some extent, sensitive to barometric pressure and these so-called weatherfish become quite active just ahead of stormy weather. Members of the Cottidae family, such as the miller's thumb *(Cottus gobio)*, are often found sheltering beneath or behind rocks in fast-flowing streams.

Extreme coloration is found in male members of the darter group, *(Etheostoma* spp.), especially during breeding time, when bright reds and blues are seen. However, at other times they may be very hard to spot, as their otherwise nondescript colours hide them very effectively against the similarly coloured substrate. These fish move rapidly in short sharp 'hops', using their caudal and pectoral fins for propulsion.

Of all the bottom-dwelling fish, some are worthy of mention (and careful consideration) for almost the same reason – size. The sailfin sucker *(Myxocyprinus asiaticus)* is an

Above: The rainbow darter (Etheostoma caeruleum) *spends all of its time on the substrate, over which it progresses in leaps and hops in its search for food.*

interesting-looking fish, often with vertical black-and-rust-coloured stripes, and a very high 'sail-like' dorsal fin. When seen as a young fish at the point of sale, hardly anything alerts you to the fact that it will grow very large, very quickly.

Intrigued, perhaps, by their form and delicate barbels, people have long been fascinated by catfish. They are often seen as grey or black juveniles in dealers' tanks and appear quite harmless. However, like the foregoing species, growth rates are high and the fish often display predatory instincts (usually at night). For those wishing to keep a catfish in a large aquarium or outside pond, it is vital to exercise extreme caution, especially with regard to other pond or tank inmates. (A fast-growing catfish will have no regard at all for the existing fish – except to make a meal of them!) If you are determined to proceed, then the black bullhead *(Ictalurus melas)* and the channel catfish *(I. punctatus)* might conceivably just fit the bill. However, as both grow to well over 5m (16ft), you might wish to reconsider.

Right: *In the wild, the stone loach (Barbatula barbatula) can be found under stones in fast-flowing streams. In captivity, it needs well-aerated water and cool conditions. It likes worm-type foods.*

Below: *This highly intimidating view of the miller's thumb (Cottus gobio) is made more so by the stiffly held, large pectoral fins, which add apparent 'size' to the fish to deter predators. It can itself be predatory in captivity.*

Below: The diminutive medaka (Oryzias sp.) can withstand very low temperatures, and has even been observed swimming quite happily beneath the ice on the pond in the very depths of winter.

Right: With its high dorsal fin and striking coloration, there is no doubting the visual attractions of the juvenile sailfin sucker (Myxocyprinus asiaticus). *Problems arise when its unsuspecting owner finds out just how large (and how quickly) it grows! 30cm (12in) is not an unusual size for this species. Just as disappointing is the fact that the attractive juvenile colours fade with age; the adult fish takes on a very uninteresting grey coloration. It is often offered for sale as a tropical species, as it is imported along with them fairly regularly.*

A GUIDE TO CLASSIFICATION

There are more than 20,000 individual 'sorts' of living fish currently known to science, plus many more that have become extinct. How can we classify them all into a clearly understandable system? Here we explain how it works.

Which one is it?

Where more than one species exists in a genus, such as with this *Umbra pygmaea*, a form of listing is necessary to differentiate between them.

How would you go about listing all the fishes in the world? Shapes and colours would seem to be a feasible proposal, but just imagine how many 'silver' and 'cylindrical' ones you would end up with!

By far the best way is to study the fish's anatomy and describe it using some basic parameters: scale and fin-ray counts are a must, plus any other physical characteristics you care to note, such as body depth, head to body proportions, snout length, mouth position, number of barbels, eye diameter, caudal peduncle length

and depth, and so on. Then, you will need to make note of where it was found, and in what water conditions. You may even open up its stomach to discern what it had recently eaten to establish its regular diet. A colour photograph or drawing would also help, especially as the fish's colours would probably have faded by the time it reached the laboratory for further dissection and more a detailed internal study.

Once all the necessary information has been gathered, a dossier could be recorded and entered into a library of information. If it is thought to be a newly discovered species then a further task lies ahead before it can be named for science. What if there is already another description of the fish on record to refute the claim of a new species? Now you need a

Below: Where cultivated forms have been developed in the aquarium (here gold and silver bitterlings), they are still the same species but may be called 'colour strains' to distinguish them.

standardized and unambiguous way of describing fish (or any other living thing, for that matter).

The Linnean system

Carl von Linné (1707-1778) was a Swedish systematist and it was his 'binominal' nomenclature (two-naming system) that revolutionized (and simplified) scientific record-keeping. His *Systema Naturae* published in 1758 used this method of naming in its 10th edition. Linnaeus, as he came to be universally known, gave every living thing a two-part name: the first part was the generic name, the second the 'trivial' or specific name. The generic (or genus) name always begins with a

capital letter, the specific name with a small letter. As a further record, the name of the describer of any species (not always the discoverer) together with the date of the description followed the scientific name. *Carassius carassius* Linnaeus 1758 or *Elassoma evergladei* Jordan 1884 are typical examples. Often you will find that the name following the scientific name is in brackets. This means that the specific name was first applied to a previous (since amended) generic name.

Incidentally, there are strict laws of precedence within the naming process. The best known (and most used) is that of priority; the name first given takes precedence over any that may be given at a later date. This is quite likely to happen if a wide-ranging species is 'discovered' by two separate people, each one ignorant of the other. In this case, it is the earliest given name that takes precedent. It is easy to see how many fishes could be given a similar specific name – say, *fasciatus* (barred) – but no two different fish can ever be given the same generic and specific name combination; there is nothing to prevent different genera having members with the same perfectly descriptive specific name; hence, *Carassius auratus*, *Gobius auratus* and *Melanochromis auratus*,

Below: The Crucian carp, Carassius carassius, *is a direct relative of the goldfish, which was once named* Carassius carassius auratus – *a colour variant or subspecies.*

A typical classification

PHYLUM
Chordata (Animals with backbones)

CLASS
Osteichthyes (Bony fishes)

SUPER-ORDER
Teleostei (Higher bony fishes)

ORDER
Cypriniformes (Carplike fishes)

FAMILY
Cyprinidae (Cyprinids)

GENUS	SPECIES	SUBSPECIES	COMMON NAME
Carassius	*auratus*	–	Goldfish
Carassius	*auratus*	*gibelio*	Prussian carp
Carassius	*carassius*	–	Crucian carp
Cyprinus	*carpio*	–	Common carp
Cyprinus	*carpio*	–	Koi

auratus being the common description – 'gold'. In human analogous terms, generic names correspond to our surnames, with specific names being our forenames – hence Brian Smith, Brian Jones and Brian Brown; Smith, Jones and Brown are thus regarded as generic names, with Brian the common specific name to each. Of course, this does not mean that any fish cannot be reclassified into another genus should research prove it necessary.

When studying fish names, it is typical to find that often the generic name describes one of the fish's physical characteristics while the specific name may refer to a geographic location or to a person. Thus, *Elassoma evergladei*, translates as 'little body from the Everglades' and *Lepomis gibbosus* is 'scaled gill cover with humped-back.'

As a rough guide, names ending in 'ensis' are likely to be geographic descriptions, such as *brasiliensis* meaning from Brazil. Those ending in 'i' or 'ae' usually indicate an honorary naming (male or female) such as *innesi* (after Innes) or *marthae* (after Martha). One of the most commonly used name-building blocks is, of course, *ichthys*, the Greek word for fish.

GLOSSARY

If you have been puzzled by some of the words used in the book, this quick reference guide will put your mind at rest. Of course, some of the descriptions are necessarily short and you should refer to other sources for more details.

Adipose fin Small extra fin between the dorsal fin and the caudal fin.

Aeration The movement of water (to aid gaseous exchanges) created by the introduction of a supply of air into the aquarium or pond by means of an airpump or by venturi effect.

Algae Tiny, unicellular plants that may coat aquatic plants or cause a green cloudiness in the water.

Anal fin Single fin underneath the fish, similar to a ship's keel.

Barbels Group of whiskerlike growths around the mouth of, for example, catfishes and cyprinids.

Biological filter A system of filtration in which colonizing bacteria convert ammonia (NH_3) first to nitrite (NO_2) and then to nitrate (NO_3), rendering it less toxic. Ponds may have filters built 'in situ' or external units alongside. Tanks may have biological filtration as an 'undergravel' system or in an external fluidized bed unit. Biological filtration also occurs in 'over-dirty' canister-type conventional filters. Cleaning destroys this action.

Blanketweed Fast-growing, silklike algae that becomes a nuisance due to rampant growth.

Catfishes Bottom-dwelling fishes, quite recognizable by their well-developed barbels.

Caudal fin The tail, or single fin, at the rear end of a fish.

Caudal peduncle Narrow part of the fish's body that connects to the caudal fin.

Chromatophores Colour pigmentation cells in the skin.

Conditioning The bringing of fishes into a prime state of health for breeding.

Countershading The basic coloration pattern of fish: dark on top, shading down to silver below.

Ctenoid scale Scale with comblike teeth on its rear edge.

Cycloid scale Round, smooth scale.

Demersal Heavier than water.

Above: Estuarine waters pose problems for fish. Varying water levels bring varying degrees of salinity as well as allowing regular danger from predators.

Dorsal Pertaining to the fish's back.

Dorsal fin Single fin on the top of the fish's body. Some species have more than one.

Erythrophores Red pigment cells.

Estuarine Region where freshwater rivers meet the salt water of the sea. Salinity levels may vary due to regular tidal changes.

Fancy goldfish Any of the cultivated varieties of the common goldfish, especially the twintailed forms.

Fertile Describes sexually mature fishes, or eggs containing developing fish embryos.

129

Filter Device for cleaning and purifying the aquarium or pond water by mechanical, chemical or biological means.

Filter medium Any material used as a trapping, straining, adsorptive or bacteria-colonizing device in a filter system for pond or aquarium.

Fins Propelling and steering organs of a fish, usually seven in number: anal, dorsal, caudal (adipose, if present), pectoral (2), and pelvic or ventral (2).

Fright substance Chemical substance excreted by injured fish, especially minnows, that sends alarm signals to the rest of the shoal.

Fry The young of a fish.

Ganoid scale Four-sided, smooth enamel-like scale equipped with tiny teeth. Seen on primitive fishes.

Genus (plural Genera) Individual group within a family, containing one or more species.

Gill rakers Fibrous filamentous network ahead of the gills to strain out solid materials from the water. Used by plankton feeders to collect microscopic foods.

Gills Organs by which the fish extracts oxygen from the water and expels carbon dioxide and ammonia.

Guanin Crystalline waste substance often deposited beneath the skin in cyprinids, rather than being excreted. Gives the fish its metallic shine.

Hand-stripping *See* Stripping.

Below: Newly hatched fish fry are very hard to spot amongst the aquatic plants in the aquarium; they look like small splinters of glass as they cling to the tank.

Hermaphrodite Having functional male and female sexual organs.

Hood Tank lid housing the lighting equipment. Often acts as a reflector as well as a protective cover.

Infertile Not able to reproduce. Often applied to fish eggs that do not produce young.

Iridocytes Cells containing guanin, a reflective material beneath the skin. Sometimes called guanophores.

Lateral line A vibration-sensing system that appears as a row of tiny holes along the sides of the fish.

Marine Pertaining to sea water.

Matt A scale type in goldfish that has no guanin layer beneath the scale.

Melanophores Black pigment cells.

Metallic A scale type in goldfish in which there is a layer of reflecting guanin beneath the scale.

Milt The fertilizing fluid of the male fish containing the sperm.

Myotomes Muscle segments along the flanks of the fish.

Nacreous A scale type in goldfish with less guanin than 'metallic' but more than 'matt.'

Neuromasts Vibration-sensing cells lying beneath the skin as part of the lateral line system.

Operculum External covering to the gills. Also called gill cover.

Osmoregulation Method by which a fish regulates, or balances, its internal salt and water content against that of the surrounding water.

Ovipositor Tube for depositing eggs. It is extended at breeding times by the female of some fishes, especially obvious in the bitterling.

Oxygenators Fast-growing plants that give off surplus oxygen during hours of sunlight. Excessive growth will cause oxygen depletion at night and could suffocate fish.

Parthenogenesis Reproduction from an egg without fertilization.

Pectoral fins Paired fins immediately behind the fish's gills.

Pelagic Lighter than water; usually used to refer to fertilized eggs that drift after spawning.

Pelvic fins Paired fins on the fish's ventral surface, ahead of the anal fin. Also known as the ventral fins.

pH Unit of measurement of the water's acidity or alkalinity. In a freshwater aquarium, the optimum pH level is 6.5-7.5. In a marine aquarium, pH is 7.9-8.5.

Pharyngeal teeth Teeth in the throat of cyprinid species used to grind up food against a horny pad at the base of the skull.

Photosynthesis Process by which green plants under illumination use carbon dioxide and nutrients to build sugars and starches within the green cells, and give off surplus oxygen.

Piscinae 'Aquariums' or fish-holding tanks built in Roman times.

Piscivore Fish-eating.

Power filter Filter system in which a high water-turnover rate is achieved by means of a small electrically driven water pump.

Quarantine The isolation of new fishes (and plants) in case of disease before adding them to the main aquarium or pond.

Scales Thin bony plates covering the skin of the fish.

Scutes Thick, armoured plates, instead of scales, found in sturgeons.

Shoal Naturally occurring congregation of one species of fish, usually for mutual protection, but also for mass spawnings.

Spawning Breeding.

Spawning tank A separate aquarium especially prepared for the purpose of housing a breeding pair (or shoal) of adult fishes, and where the young fry may be raised.

Species Classification term used to denote allied groups of fishes within a genus.

Spines Thickened fin rays or bony extensions to gill plates that offer the fish offensive or defensive capabilities. A thickened fin ray is usually indicative of the male fish.

Standard body length The length of the fish, excluding the caudal fin.

Stew-ponds Middle English term derived from the French 'estui', from estoier meaning 'to confine'.

Stripping (Hand-stripping) The manual process of removing eggs from a female fish and milt from a male fish. Usually practised in fancy goldfish culture.

Substrate The medium covering the base of an aquarium, such as gravel.

Swimbladder Organ inside the fish's body that automatically adjusts buoyancy.

Tail The caudal fin.

Tubercles Small white pimples that develop on the gill covers and pectoral fins of male goldfish and other cyprinids during the breeding season.

Turbidity Impaired clarity of water, usually by suspended detritus stirred up by water currents or movements of fish.

Undergravel filter Filtration system that uses the aquarium gravel as a bacterial bed. Also referred to as a biological filter.

Variety Fishes of the same species, in which the colour patterns or finnage have been developed and stabilized by selective breeding programmes. The term also applies to fish that may exist in nature as local variants.

Ventral fins *See* Pelvic fins.

Xanthophores Yellow pigment cells.

Above: These beautiful varieties of goldfish have been developed by breeding and would not be found in nature. They are best seen in the home aquarium.

INDEX

Page numbers in **bold** indicate major entries, *italics* refer to captions and annotations; plain type indicates other text entries.

A

Acipenser spp. 27, 61
Acipenseridae family *49*
Alburnus alburnus 34
Algae 83, 84, 88, 93
  blanketweed 84
Alopias vulpinus 61
Anglerfish 61
Anguilla spp. 74
Anodonta spp. 70
Anus 39
Aquarium 13, 76, 77, 85, 86-95, 96
  filter sponge medium 86
  filtration 86-89
    biological 88
    external power filter 86, 87, *87*
    internal power filter 86, *86*
  fish 85, **96-123**
  lighting 88, *88*
  planting the 93

plants 88
  oxgenating *93*
  plastic 90, *90*, *91*, *93*
  setting up 76
  stocking levels 89
  temperature 89, *89*
  unheated 12
Arum lilies 83

B

Barbatula barbatula *120*
Barbels 35, *35*, *54*, 55, 60, 61, *102*, *103*, 119
Basses 116
Bichirs 26
Bitterling 70, *70*, 106, *106*
  gold *125*
  silver *125*
Bleak 34
Blennies 14
Blennius pholis *43*
Blood 38, 40, 41, 42
  circulation *38*, 39
Body 22, 24, 26
  caudal peduncle 24
  pattern 22
  shape 16, *23*, 24, 96
  size 16, 21

Body coverings 26
  bony plates (scutes) 27, *49*, 55, *56*
  scales 26, *26*, 27, 28, 30, *31*, 48, 49, 50, *96*, 98
  ctenoid 26, *27*
  cycloid 26, *26*, 27, *27*
  ganoid 26, *27*
  matt 30, *31*, 96
  metallic 30, *31*, 96
  nacreous 30, *31*, 96
  skin 26, *26*, *30*
  iridocytes (guanophores) 30
Brain *33*, 36
Breeding 11, *13*, 25, **64-75**, 97, *133*
  koi 18, 21
  newly hatched fry *130*
  spawning ropes 68
  stock 18
  tubercles 25, 66, 67, 110, 111
Burbot 59

C

Camouflage 29
Carassius auratus 18, 96, 126,

CREDITS

The publishers would like to thank the following photographers for providing images, credited here by page number and position: B(Bottom), T(Top), C(Centre), BL(Bottom left), etc.

Ardea London: 120(B)
M P & C Piednoir/Aqua Press: 23(B), 53, 54-55(B), 68, 94-95, 96, 116-117(T), 119(T), 133
Dave Bevan: 10, 22, 31(BR), 43, 54(T), 57(BR), 60(T,B), 67, 76, 103(B), 110-111(B), 113(B), 114-115(T,B), 125
The Bridgeman Art Library: 17(The Month of April, Book of Hours, c.1540 by Simon Bening (1483-1561) Victoria & Albert Museum, London), 18(Selection of Oriental porcelain, pair of cloisonne vases with carp and wisteria decoration; Imari charger and ovoid jar, celadon double gourd ewer, Bonhams, London), 19(1973-22c Shin Bijin (True Beauties) depicting a woman holding a goldfish bowl, from a series of 36, modelled on an earlier series by Utamaro (1753-1806) 19th century (woodblock) by Toyohara Chinanobu (1838-1912) Oriental Museum, Durham University, Durham)
Bruce Coleman Collection: 24(BC, Jane Burton), 39(Robert Maier), 64(Dr. Eckart Pott), 65(Jane Burton), 69(T,C,B, Kim Taylor), 70-71(Kim Taylor), 73(B, Charles & Sandra Hood), 108(T, Jane Burton)
Derek Cattani: 20-21(T), 20(BL), 78-79, 82, 102, 104-105(T)
C M Dixon: 16
John Feltwell (Wildlife Matters): Copyright page, 12
Frank Lane Picture Agency: 126(W. Meinderts/Foto Natura)
Dick Mills: 105(BR), 109(T)
Heather Angel/Natural Visions: 44-45, 47, 73(T)
Aaron Norman: 23(T), 34-35(B), 58-59(T), 62-63, 101(T,B), 107(C), 108-109(B), 112-113(T), 112(B), 116-117(B), 122-123, 124
Arend van den Nieuwenhuizen: 51, 100(T)
Photomax (Max Gibbs): Title page, 28, 49, 72, 97(C,B), 98(TL,BL), 99, 106, 107(T), 110-111(T), 118-119(B), 120-121(T), 121(B), 130
Geoffrey Rogers © Interpet Publishing: 25, 26, 30(TL,TR), 31(TR, CR), 37(T), 92(CL,BR), 103(T), 104(L)
Fred Rosenzweig: 100(B)
Sue Scott: 13, 14-15, 29, 50, 52, 56-57(T), 74-75(B), 75(TR), 129

The artwork illustrations have been prepared by Phil Holmes and Stuart Watkinson and are © Interpet Publishing.

ACKNOWLEDGMENTS

The publishers acknowledge that the illustrations featured in this book have been based on the following sources: *Vertebrate Life* by F. Harvey Pough, Christine M. Janis and John B. Heiser, published by Prentice-Hall Inc., New Jersey, 1999. *The Biology of Fishes* by Q. Bone, N.B. Marshall and J.H.S. Blaxter, published by Stanley Thornes (Publishers) Ltd., Cheltenham, 1999. *The Vertebrate Eye* by G.L. Walls, published by Hafner, New York, 1963. The publishers would like to thank the following for their help in the preparation of this book: Heaver Tropics, Ash, Sevenoaks, Kent; The Koi Waterlife Centre, Southfleet, Kent